Monarchy or Republic?

ISSUES

(formerly Issues for the Nineties)

Volume 37

Editor

Craig Donnellan

Independence

Educational Publishers
Cambridge

First published by Independence
PO Box 295
Cambridge CB1 3XP
England

© Craig Donnellan 1998

British Library Cataloguing in Publication Data
Monarchy or Republic? – (Issues Series)
I. Donnellan, Craig II. Series
321.8'6

ISBN 1 86168 070 8

Printed in Great Britain
City Print Ltd
Milton Keynes

Typeset by
Claire Boyd

Cover
The illustration on the front cover is by
The Attic Publishing Co.

CONTENTS

Introduction

Monarcy or Republic? is the thirty-seventh volume in the series: **Issues**. The aim of this series is to offer up-to-date information about important issues in our world.

Monarcy or Republic? looks at the current debate about the future of the monarchy.

The information comes from a wide variety of sources and includes:
Government reports and statistics
Newspaper reports and features
Magazine articles and surveys
Literature from lobby groups
and charitable organisations.

It is hoped that, as you read about the many aspects of the issues explored in this book, you will critically evaluate the information presented. It is important that you decide whether you are being presented with facts or opinions. Does the writer give a biased or an unbiased report? If an opinion is being expressed, do you agree with the writer?

Monarcy or Republic? offers a useful starting-point for those who need convenient access to information about the many issues involved. However, it is only a starting-point. At the back of the book is a list of organisations which you may want to contact for further information.

*****

The monarchy

Information from Charter 88

The UK has one of the oldest and most powerful monarchies in the world. While some other democratic countries still have monarchies – such as Spain, Norway, and Belgium – they all have written constitutions which spell out what powers those monarchies should have. And the people living there are citizens of the country who swear loyalty to the constitution rather than to the monarch.

In the UK the situation is more complex. We do not have a written constitution so much of our monarchy's powers are based on custom and not very clearly defined. Also, we are not citizens of the UK but subjects of the monarch of the UK. The Crown is the only institution in the UK that has the right to rule. Even though much of its power is in practice exercised by Parliament the Queen still has personal constitutional powers.

This information sets out a brief history of the UK monarchy, what powers it currently has, and what options for change different groups are arguing for. There are other factsheets on connected topics like the House of Lords, the Commons, and the legislative process.

History

Parts of the UK have had monarchies since early times. In 1649 King Charles I was executed and Britain became a Republic for eleven years. The monarchy was restored in 1660. But later there was disagreement about what powers it should have and whether a Catholic could be monarch. In 1688, the Catholic James II abdicated and Queen Mary and her husband, William of Orange, were asked to be joint monarchs.

In 1689 William and Mary signed a document which set out limits to their powers to interfere with Parliament. It also set out that the monarch must be head of the Church of England. The document was called the Bill of Rights, though it was about Parliament's rights rather than the rights of the people.

Political powers of the monarchy now

In practice the monarchy's powers have reduced further since 1688. The situation now is roughly as follows

1. The oath of loyalty

Public servants and members of the armed forces and the police swear an oath of loyalty to the monarch. In countries where the people are sovereign, they swear an oath to uphold the constitution – the document containing the agreed rules of government.

2. The right to be consulted, 'advise and warn'

The monarchy has the right to advise and warn the government of the day. The Prime Minister meets the monarch on a regular basis. However the proceedings of the meetings are secret.

3. The Queen's Speech

The Queen visits the House of Lords at the start of each parliamentary session – usually once a year – to read the Queen's Speech. Members of the Commons come to listen. The speech describes visits she will make and the major Bills 'Her Majesty's Government' will be introducing.

So the speech is a symbol that the monarch does still have some presence in Parliament. But it is the Government that writes the speech, so in that sense it does not show the monarch exercising any real power.

4. The power to enact legislation

A Bill does not become law unless it is approved by the monarch. No monarch has refused to sign a bill since 1707 but the right still exists.

5. The Royal Prerogative

Like the right to tell Parliament what Bills will be introduced that year, the monarch has other rights or prerogatives, which have in reality been given to the Government of the day. The main Royal Prerogative Powers are as follows:

The power to appoint and award honours

The decision about who to give honours, peerages or bishoprics to is made by the government but is done in the monarch's name and she conducts the relevant ceremonies. The government also tells the monarch who to appoint as Ministers, judges, magistrates, and other holders of public office.

The power to choose the Prime Minister
When the need arises, the monarch calls the leader of one of the political parties and invites him or her to form a government. By convention, the monarch usually calls the leader of the party that won the most seats at the election. There would be an outcry if she didn't! However, it is possible that if no one party has a clear majority of seats, the monarch will have to exercise some discretion.

The power to approve the dissolution of Parliament
The monarch decides when to dissolve Parliament and call an election, on the Prime Minister's advice. It would cause an outcry if the monarch refused to do what the Prime Minister asked. However, an election might be refused if Parliament could form another government without one.

The power to declare war
The government, using the Royal Prerogative, can decide when to declare war or commit resources to a war. Because the government is still responsible to Parliament when exercising prerogative powers, it does recognise the importance of getting Parliament to approve its decisions after it has made them.

For example, the government asked Parliament to approve its declaration of war in the Gulf and commitment of resources there, but not till four days after fighting had begun. In that instance, Parliament agreed that the government had made the right decision. However there could be a crisis one day if Parliament did not approve a prerogative decision the monarch and government had already taken.

The power to sign treaties
The government can sign treaties without checking with Parliament, though it should get Parliamentary approval afterwards. That is one reason why there was such argument during the debates on the Maastricht Treaty in 1993.

The government had, using the monarch's prerogative powers, already signed the Maastricht Treaty. But it wanted to get Parliamentary approval, and at one stage it looked

as if a revolt by Conservative backbenchers would prevent this. At this stage members of the government stressed that because of the Royal Prerogative they did not actually need Parliamentary approval. This caused great offence to some MPs and was the subject of fierce constitutional argument – when a constitution is not written down such arguments are more likely to happen, because any decision is more open to interpretation. In the event, the government was not defeated on the crucial motion, they had to use a 'Vote of Confidence' mechanism to ensure success – so the confrontation between government and Parliament over the extent of the Royal Prerogative did not occur.

Some people say that, while all countries allow their governments some prerogative powers, only in the UK are they so extensive and open to interpretation. Some experts believe that the prestige of the monarchy allows the government to get away with more use of prerogative powers than they would otherwise be able to.

6. Other royal powers
The monarch has great wealth. She is head of state, so meets many other representatives of foreign governments. She is also head of the Commonwealth, which is an association of some of the countries the UK used to rule as colonies. And in states of emergency the Queen can govern through the Privy Council without reference to Parliament. In general it is said that the Queen's influence is greater than her official powers.

Options for reform
1. Keep things as they are
The arguments for keeping the monarchy as it is are:
- people in the UK value the monarchy as part of their history the monarchy provides stability
- no elected or appointed person could perform the ceremonial roles as well as the monarch does
- the colour and tradition provided by the monarchy are a great tourist attraction
- the fact that the monarch performs the ceremonial role allows the Prime Minister to concentrate on more important tasks
- the monarchy is above party politics, which is right for a head of state
- as far as the royal prerogative powers are concerned these are not in reality exercised by the monarch but by elected politicians
- if widespread changes were made, for example to the monarch's power to award peerages, then other sweeping changes to the constitution, like reform of the Lords, would have to be made and there would be too much upheaval
- the Church of England is a positive force in UK life and it and the monarch's leadership of it should be maintained.

2. Introduce minor reforms
Some people argue that minor reforms should be introduced which would not require much constitutional upheaval. For example, the number of royals receiving public money from the civil list could be reduced, and style aspects of the monarchy – such as the number and age of its palaces – could be scaled down to make the monarchy seem closer to the people.

3. Ceremonial monarchy
Some people argue for a ceremonial or Scandinavian style monarchy. Such monarchies are still 'head of state' in that they perform ceremonial roles meeting other heads of state. But they do not have any royal prerogative powers – and do not even pretend to have a role in parliament.

There are no official state churches like the Church of England.

Because such countries have written constitutions which set out the powers of Parliament and rights of the people then people swear an oath of loyalty to the constitution not the monarch. In Sweden, for example, the constitution makes the people themselves sovereign and the king as head of state has no constitutional powers. They also do not have other hereditary institutions with political power, like the House of Lords.

4. Republic

The arguments in favour of abolishing the monarchy are:

- the monarch is unelected, unrepresentative and unaccountable to the people, who should be sovereign
- the hereditary principle is elitist and sends the wrong signals to society. It seems to say that what

is important is what family you are born into rather than how far you can get on your own merits

- none of the half way solutions such as a constitutional monarchy will provide the UK with the modern constitution it needs
- hereditary office restricts the freedom of monarchs to live lives of their own choosing

Some republicans believe the monarchy and hereditary elements like the Lords could be abolished (and Church of England disestablished) while the UK still kept its parliamentary system of government. In other words the Prime Minister would become head of state.

Others argue that after the monarchy is abolished the UK should elect a President to be ceremonial head of state. Also the UK should develop a written constitution which introduces a Bill of Rights for the people, abolishes the Lords (to replace it with an elected senate), and sets up a constitutional court to check that the constitution is upheld.

There are other models:

In France an elected President shares the powers of government with a Prime Minister who is leader of the largest party in parliament. In the USA an elected President also holds all government (executive) power. During the Citizens' Enquiry, people were asked to fill in questionnaires on these issues.

• The above is an extract from the Charter 88 web site. See page 43 for full details.

© *Charter 88*
June, 1998

The Queen's role in the modern state

The Queen is a constitutional monarch: in other words, she is bound by rules and conventions and cannot rule in an arbitrary way. Limits began to be placed on the powers of the monarch as far back as 1215 when the barons forced King John to recognise in Magna Carta that they had certain rights. The constitutional monarchy we know today developed in the eighteenth and nineteenth centuries, as day-to-day power came to be exercised by Ministers in Cabinet, deriving their authority from Parliaments elected from a steadily widening electorate.

The essence of the monarchy today is that the Queen is politically impartial. On almost all matters she acts on the advice of the Government of the day. The tasks of making laws, administering justice, and governing and defending the country are carried out by others in the Queen's name. The monarch thus symbolises the permanence and stability of the nation, which transcends the ebb and flow of party politics.

Queen in Parliament

This is the formal title of the British legislature, which consists of the Sovereign, the House of Lords and the House of Commons. The Commons, a majority of whom normally support the government of the day, has the dominant political power.

The essence of the monarchy today is that the Queen is politically impartial. On almost all matters she acts on the advice of the Government of the day

---

As constitutional monarch, the Sovereign is required, on the advice of Ministers, to assent to all Bills. The Royal Assent (that is, consenting to a measure becoming law) has not been refused since 1707. The role of the Sovereign in the enactment of legislation is today purely formal, although the Queen has the right to be consulted, to encourage and to warn.

The Queen in Parliament is most clearly demonstrated in the State Opening of Parliament, when the Queen opens Parliament in person, and addresses both Houses in the Queen's Speech. This speech, drafted by the Government and not by the Queen, outlines the Government's policy for the coming session of Parliament and indicates forthcoming legislation. Each session, therefore, begins with the Queen's Speech, and the Houses cannot start their public business until the Speech has been read.

Queen and Prime Minister

The Queen retains certain residual powers, notably to appoint a Prime Minister, and to decide whether or not to grant a dissolution of Parliament. The Prime Minister is normally the leader of the party which has a majority in Parliament, but there could still be exceptional circumstances when the Queen might need to exercise the discretion she still retains to ensure that her Government is carried on.

These days, however, the Queen's influence is mainly informal. She has a right and a duty to express her views on government matters to the Prime Minister at their weekly audiences, but these meetings – and all communications between the monarch and her Government – remain strictly confidential. Having expressed her views, the Queen abides by the advice of her Ministers.

Queen and Privy Council

The Privy Council is the oldest form of legislative assembly still functioning; its origins date from the Norman Kings' Court, which met in private. Until the seventeenth century, the king and his Council were the Government, with Parliament's role limited to voting funds. Today, the Privy Council has limited, formal executive functions which retain some significance.

On the advice of the Privy Council, the Queen formally approves a large number of Orders in Council (which, by Acts of Parliament, enact subordinate legislation ranging from constitutions of dependent territories to international pollution). The Queen also approves Proclamations (formal notices which cover areas such as the dissolution of Parliament, coinage and dates of certain Bank Holidays). The Privy Council also has certain judicial functions.

There are 400 Privy Councillors, consisting of all members of the Cabinet, a number of middle-ranking government ministers, leaders of the opposition parties in both Houses of Parliament, senior judges and some appointments from the Commonwealth.

Queen and the law/judiciary
Sovereign as 'Fount of Justice'

The rendering of justice is one of the oldest of royal functions. From late Anglo-Saxon times, the concept of the Sovereign as the 'Fount of Justice' grew in importance as it helped to ensure that a single system of justice prevailed over competing local, civil and ecclesiastical jurisdictions. Ethelbert's reign (560-616) saw the first law code written in the vernacular; kings such as Alfred the Great (reigned 871-99) extended the law codes by codifying community custom, administrative regulations and ancient law. Successive kings preserved and adapted the body of English laws which had been accepted by the community and which past kings had published, and case law supplemented these law codes.

This accumulated legislative power placed responsibilities on the king as a dispenser of justice to ensure order and punish crime. From William the Conqueror (reigned 1066-87) onwards, royal justice was more effectively enforced by the king's appointment of local sheriffs, travelling justices and other officials to administer justice in the Sovereign's name throughout the kingdom. A chronicler of 1179 wrote of Henry II (reigned 1154-89): 'he appointed wise men from his kingdom and later sent them through the regions of the kingdom assigned to them to execute justice among the people . . . This he did in order that the coming of public officials of authority throughout the shires might strike terror into the hearts of wrongdoers.'

The royal courts were therefore at the centre of the administration of justice in both civil and criminal cases, and sovereigns themselves took an active part in their own courts, with the king sometimes presiding over the proceedings. By the fifteenth century, the central courts had settled at Westminster, and the Courts of Justice remained housed at Westminster Hall (built in 1097 and renovated in 1394) until 1882.

However, there were limits to royal enforcement of justice or 'the king's peace'. These limits included the geographical distance of the more remote shires (particularly on the troubled borders of the Welsh Marches and Scotland), the independent jurisdiction of 'palatine counties' (where royal powers were granted in franchise to an individual), ecclesiastical jurisdictions and, above all, the Sovereign's reliance on local barons and gentry to uphold the law in the regions – which was liable to break down in times of civil war.

Moreover, as Parliament's legislative role grew and day-to-day power came to be exercised by Ministers in Cabinet, so the Sovereign's role in actually administering justice declined. The Bill of Rights (1689) (in Scotland, the Claim of Right in the same year) confirmed the fundamental constitutional principle that the Sovereign no longer had any right to administer justice. The Sovereign's responsibilities regarding the judiciary also waned – under the Act of Settlement (1701), judges were to hold office during good behaviour rather than by the Sovereign's will. (Judges can be removed by the Sovereign on the advice of Ministers, either following an address presented by both Houses of Parliament or without an address in cases of official misconduct or conviction of a serious offence.) The Act therefore established judicial independence.

Royal finances

Sources of funding

The four sources of funding of the Queen, or officials of the Royal Household acting on Her Majesty's behalf, are:

- the Civil List
- the Grants-in-Aid for upkeep of Royal Palaces and for Royal travel
- the Privy Purse
- the Queen's personal wealth and income.

The Civil List

The Civil List is the sum provided by Parliament to meet the official expenses of the Queen's Household so that Her Majesty can fulfil her role as Head of State and Head of the Commonwealth. It is not in any sense 'pay' for the Queen.

The Civil List dates back to the restoration of the monarchy in 1660, but the current system was created on the accession of George III in 1760, when it was decided that the whole cost of civil government should be provided by Parliament in return for the surrender of the hereditary revenues (principally the annual income of the Crown Estate) by the King for the duration of the reign. Revenue from the Crown Estate amounted to £103 million in 1996-97 and this was paid to the Treasury.

About 70 per cent of Civil List expenditure goes to pay the salaries of staff working directly for the Queen. Their duties include dealing with State papers, organising public engagements and arranging meetings and receptions undertaken by the Queen. The Civil List also meets the costs of functions such as the Royal Garden Parties (Her Majesty entertains over 48,000 people each year) and official entertainment during State Visits.

The Civil List is set by Parliament as a fixed annual amount of £7.9 million for a period of up to 10 years. The Household is currently succeeding in containing Civil List expenditure within inflation, however, and the resulting surplus is being carried forward to reduce the amount of the Civil List for the next 10-year period.

The budget for each year's projected net Civil List spending is reviewed by the Treasury, which audits the accounts and verifies that the Household's financial management is in line with best practice. Details of expenditure are published.

The Grants-in-Aid

Property services

Parliament, through the Department of Culture, Media and Sport, provides a Grant-in-Aid annually to the Royal Household. The money is used for the upkeep of the palaces occupied by members of the Royal family, and used for official purposes. These are Buckingham Palace, St James's Palace and Clarence House, Marlborough House Mews, parts of Kensington Palace, Windsor Castle and related buildings and Hampton Court Mews and Paddocks. Also included are the Queen's Gallery at Buckingham Palace and properties available for residential use, mainly by staff and pensioners. Costs of the Historic Royal Palaces or Un-occupied Palaces are not the responsibility of the Royal Household. The Historic Royal Palaces Agency (an agency of the Department of Culture, Media and Sport) looks after the Unoccupied Palaces, which include the Tower of London, Hampton Court and the State Apartments at Kensington Palace.

Approximately 75 per cent of funds are spent on the maintenance of the buildings. The rest goes toward utilities, fire, health and safety services, non-domestic rates, administration and maintenance of gardens.

Accounts are published and presented to Parliament each year. In 1996-97 the Grant-in-Aid amounted to £19,609,000, but the Royal Household plans to reduce the annual sum to £15 million by the end of the decade.

Royal travel

Each year the members of the Royal Family carry out more than 2,500 official engagements in the United Kingdom and overseas; hitherto the travel costs involved have been met directly by government departments.

From April 1997, the Royal Household receives a Grant-in-Aid

WINDSOR CASTLE
ADMISSION CHARGES
GO TOWARDS
MAINTENANCE

from Parliament, through the Department of the Environment, Transport and the Regions to pay for Royal travel. The Grant-in-Aid amounts to £19.5 million, including £16.5 million for flying on official engagements by 32 (The Royal) Squadron. An annual report will be published. The Grant-in-Aid will be used to buy air and rail travel, using the services of the Royal Train, the RAF's 32 (The Royal) Squadron and suitable commercial providers.

The Privy Purse

The principal responsibility of the Privy Purse Office is to manage the Sovereign's private income from the Duchy of Lancaster. This amounted to £5.32 million before tax for the year to 31 March 1997. The Duchy is a landed estate held in trust for the Sovereign since 1399.

While the income is private the Queen uses the larger part of it to meet official expenses incurred by other members of the Royal Family. Only the Queen, Queen Elizabeth the Queen Mother and the Duke of Edinburgh receive payments from

Parliament which are not reimbursed by the Queen.

The Chancellor of the Duchy of Lancaster, who is the equivalent of the chairman of the trustees, has in recent years normally been a Government Minister although this is not a requirement.

The Queen's personal wealth and income

The Queen's personal income, derived from her personal investment portfolio, is used to meet private expenditure. Her Majesty's private funds, as for any other individual, remain a private matter, but the Lord Chamberlain said in 1993 that estimates of £100 million and upwards were 'grossly overstated'.

The Queen owns Balmoral and Sandringham, both inherited from her father. She also owns the stud at Sandringham (with a small amount of land in Hampshire), West Ilsley Stables and Sunninghill Park, home of the Duke of York. Income derived from public access to Balmoral and Sandringham goes to charity and towards meeting the costs of managing the properties. Her Majesty owns no property outside the United Kingdom.

Estimates of the Queen's wealth have often been greatly exaggerated, as they mistakenly include items which are held by the Queen as Sovereign on behalf of the nation and are not her private property. These include Royal Palaces, most of the art treasures from the Royal Collection, heirlooms in the Queen's jewellery collection and the Crown Jewels. The 'inalienable' items held by Her Majesty as Sovereign, rather than as an individual, cannot be disposed of by the Queen and must pass to her successor as Sovereign.

© Buckingham Palace Press Office
1998

The Commonwealth

Information from Buckingham Palace Press Office

The Commonwealth is a voluntary association of 54 independent countries, almost all of which were formerly under British rule. While remaining entirely responsible for their own policies, member countries choose to consult and co-operate in certain areas such as strengthening democracy by good government, promoting human rights and working for social and economic development of poorer countries. Much of the strength of the Commonwealth is derived from its non-governmental and informal links, such as teacher-training schemes, youth ministries, distance education, science and environmental projects, shared sports and arts festivals. This means that it is as much a commonwealth of peoples as of governments.

The 1.6 billion people of Commonwealth countries make up over a quarter of the world's population, and over 50 per cent of the population of the Commonwealth is under 25. The great majority of Commonwealth members are parliamentary democracies.

Trade is one of the many links between Britain and the Commonwealth. In 1996, UK exports to Commonwealth countries amounted to £18,374 million; imports were £19,819 million.

> In 1996, UK exports
> to Commonwealth
> countries amounted to
> £18,374 million

Membership of the Commonwealth has, since its beginning, been open to any independent state which was once ruled or administered by Britain or other Commonwealth countries, and recognises the Queen as Head of the Commonwealth. (In 1995, Mozambique became the first country to join which had not previously had such links with Britain.) Almost all countries, when they became independent of the United Kingdom, have chosen to join the Commonwealth but, since the link is entirely voluntary, any member can withdraw at any time, for example, the Republic of Ireland did so in 1949, as did South Africa in 1961 (subsequently rejoined in 1994). Fiji withdrew in 1987 but subsequently rejoined in 1997.

© Buckingham Palace Press Office

The Queen's role in the Commonwealth

As Head of the Commonwealth, the Queen's role is symbolic and has no constitutional functions attached to it. The monarch personally reinforces the links by which the Commonwealth joins people together from around the world. This is done through Commonwealth visits, regular contact with the Commonwealth Secretary General and his Secretariat (the Commonwealth's central organisation which co-ordinates many Commonwealth activities and which is based in London) and Heads of Government, attending the Commonwealth Day Observance in London, broadcasting her annual Christmas and Commonwealth Day messages, acting as patron for Commonwealth cultural events and often attending the Commonwealth Games to open or close them.

During her reign, the Queen has visited every country in the Commonwealth (with the exception of Mozambique and Cameroon, who joined in 1995) and made many repeat visits, either as a multiple visit (e.g. Anguilla, Dominica, Guyana, Belize, Cayman Islands, Jamaica, Bahamas and Bermuda in February/March 1994) or to one country (such as Canada in June/July 1997, which included the celebration of Canada's National Day). The Queen also visited India and Pakistan in October 1997, to mark the fiftieth anniversary of their independence from Britain, which led to the formation of the modern Commonwealth. One-third of the Queen's total overseas visits are to Commonwealth countries. The Duke of Edinburgh, the Prince of Wales and other members of the Royal Family also pay frequent visits to the Commonwealth.

A meeting of the Commonwealth Heads of Government (CHOGM) is usually held once every two years, at locations throughout the Commonwealth. The Queen is normally present in the host country, during which she has a series of private meetings with the Commonwealth countries' leaders. The Queen also attends a reception and dinner during the conference period at which she makes a speech. The latest CHOGM was held in October 1997 in Edinburgh, and the Queen opened it herself for the first time.

> **The Queen has become a personal link and human symbol of the Commonwealth as an international organisation**

Since 1977, Commonwealth Day has been celebrated throughout the Commonwealth on the second Monday in March; this was approved by Heads of Government as a day when children throughout the Commonwealth, for whom the day is particularly intended, would be at school.

To mark the day, The Queen broadcasts a Commonwealth Day message which, like the Christmas Message, is delivered by the Queen as Head of the Commonwealth to the peoples of the Commonwealth as a whole. These messages are unique in that they are delivered on the Queen's own responsibility, drafted without Ministerial advice.

Each year, the Queen also attends an 'Observance for Commonwealth Day' which is an inter-denominational service held in Westminster Abbey, followed by a reception hosted by the Secretary General (the Head of the Commonwealth Secretariat).

The Queen distinguishes between her various roles by using a personal flag – initial E and crown within a chaplet of roses – for use at Commonwealth meetings where the Royal Standard would be inappropriate, or by using special Standards in her various realms. The Queen, though not being part of the machinery of government in the Commonwealth, has become a personal link and human symbol of the Commonwealth as an international organisation.

© Buckingham Palace Press Office

The case for the monarchy

A monarch, as the living symbol of the nation, is more easy to identify with than a constitution or ideology.

The dignity and prestige of a monarch enhances the status of a nation.

A monarch stands above politics, not owing allegiance to any political party or group and not beholden to any business interest which might fund a presidential campaign.

A monarch is able to unite a nation by representing all races, creeds, classes and political beliefs, because a monarch does not have to curry favour for votes from any section of the community.

A monarch is almost invariably more popular than an Executive President, who can be elected by less than 50% of the electorate and may therefore represent less than half of the people. In the 1995 French presidential election the future President Chirac was not the nation's choice in the first round of voting. In Britain, governments are formed on the basis of parliamentary seats won. In the 1997 General Election the Labour Prime Minister took office with only 45% of votes cast in England, Scotland and Wales. The Queen, however, as hereditary Head of State, remains the representative of the whole nation.

Elected presidents are concerned more with their own political futures and power, and as we have seen (in Brazil for example), may use their temporary tenure to enrich themselves. Monarchs are not subject to the influences which corrupt short-term presidents. A monarch looks back on centuries of history and forward to the well-being of the entire nation under his heir. Elected

presidents in their nature devote much energy to undoing the achievements of their predecessors and setting traps for their successors. With monarchs it is the reverse: they build on the achievements of their forebears in order to strengthen the position of their successors.

A long-reigning monarch can put enormous experience at the disposal of transient political leaders. Since succeeding her father in 1952 Queen Elizabeth has had a number of Prime Ministers, the latest of whom were not even in Parliament at the time of her accession. An experienced monarch can act as a brake on over ambitious or misguided politicians, and encourage others that are less confident. The reality is often the converse of the theory: the monarch is frequently the Prime Minister's best adviser.

By retaining certain constitutional powers, or at least denying them to others, a monarch is the safeguard against civil or military dictatorship. Sir Winston Churchill said that had the Kaiser still been German Head of State after 1918, Hitler would not have come to power, or at least not remained there. In

Italy, when in 1943 he had the opportunity to do, King Victor Emmanuel removed Mussolini from office. Romania's King Michael dismissed the dictator Antonescu and transferred his country from the Axis to the Allies, for which he was decorated by the great Powers, and in Bulgaria King Boris III (although obliged to enter the war on the side of the Axis) bravely refused to persecute Bulgarian Jews and would not commit his forces outside his country's borders. Within the past few years, in both Spain and Thailand, monarchs have succeeded in defending democracy against the threat of permanent military take-over. Britain's mercifully brief period of military dictatorship coincided with its only republican experiment under Oliver Cromwell.

In the opinion of the respected Irish commentator on world affairs, Conor Cruise O'Brien, 'If constitutional monarchy were to come to an end in Britain, parliamentary democracy would probably not survive it. It is, after all, through the monarchy that parliamentary control over the armed forces is mediated and maintained.'

Monarchs, particularly those in Europe, are part of an 'extended Royal Family', facilitating links between their nations. As Burke observed, nations touch at their summits. A recent example of this was the attendance of so many members of Royal Families at the Golden Wedding celebrations for the Queen and Prince Philip. Such gatherings do more to unite the peoples of Europe than any number of treaties, protocols or directives from the European Union.

A monarch is trained from birth for the position of Head of State and even where, as after the abdication of Edward VIII, a younger brother succeeds, he too has enormous experience of his country, its people and its government. The people know who will succeed, and this certainty gives a nation invaluable continuity and stability. This also explains why it is rare for an unsuitable person to become King. There are no expensive elections as in the US where, as one pro-monarchist American says, 'we have to elect a new "Royal Family" every four years'. In the French system the President may be a member of one party, while the Prime Minister is from another, which only leads to confused government. In a monarchy there is no such confusion, for the monarch does rule in conflict with government but reigns over the whole nation.

In ceremonial presidencies the Head of State is often a former politician tainted by, and still in thrall to, his former political life and loyalties, or an academic or retired diplomat who can never have the same prestige as a monarch, and who is frequently little known inside the country, and almost always totally unknown outside it. For example, ask a German who is Britain's Head of State and a high proportion will know it is Queen Elizabeth II. Ask a Briton, or any non-German, who is Head of State of Germany, and very few will be able to answer correctly.

Aided by his immediate family, a monarch can carry out a range of duties and public engagements – ceremonial, charitable, environmental etc. – which an Executive President would never have time to

> ### A monarch is almost invariably more popular than an Executive President, who can be elected by less than 50% of the electorate and may therefore represent less than half of the people

do, and to which a ceremonial President would not add lustre.

A monarch and members of a Royal Family can become involved in a wide range of issues which are forbidden to politicians. All parties have vested interests which they cannot ignore. Vernon Bogdanor says in *The Monarchy and the Constitution*: 'A politician must inevitably be a spokesperson for only part of the nation, not the whole. A politician's motives will always be suspected. Members of the Royal Family, by contrast, because of their symbolic position, are able to speak to a much wider constituency than can be commanded by even the most popular political leader.' In a republic, then, who is there to speak out on issues where the 'here today, gone tomorrow' government is constrained from criticising its backers, even though such criticism is in the national interest?

All nations are made up of families, and it is natural that a family should be at a nation's head.

While the question of Divine Right is now obsolescent, the fact that 'there's such divinity doth hedge a King' remains true, and it is interesting to note that even today Kings are able to play a role in the spiritual life of a nation which presidents seem unable to fulfil.

It has been demonstrated that, even ignoring the enormous cost of presidential elections, a monarch as head of state is no more expensive than a president. In Britain many costs, such as the upkeep of the royal residences, are erroneously thought to be uniquely attributable to the monarchy, even though the preservation of our heritage would still be undertaken if the country were a republic! The US government has criticised the cost to the Brazilian people of maintaining their president.

Even Royal Families which are not reigning are dedicated to the service of their people, and continue to be regarded as the symbol of the nation's continuity. Prominent examples are H.R.H. the Duke of Braganza in Portugal and H.R.H. the Count of Paris in France. Royal Families forced to live in exile, such as the Yugoslav and Romanian, are often promoters of charities formed to help their countries.

© *The Monarchist League*

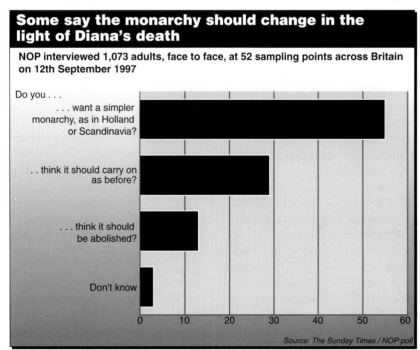

Some say the monarchy should change in the light of Diana's death

NOP interviewed 1,073 adults, face to face, at 52 sampling points across Britain on 12th September 1997

Do you . . .

. . . want a simpler monarchy, as in Holland or Scandinavia?

. . think it should carry on as before?

. . . think it should be abolished?

Don't know

0 10 20 30 40 50 60

Source: The Sunday Times / NOP poll

The press and the monarchy

The Times they are a changin' – as indeed is The Independent, The Guardian, The Observer, The Sun, The Mirror, etc. . . . Writer and broadcaster Roy Greenslade (former Daily Mirror Editor) – an active member of REPUBLIC himself – has been keeping an eye on the media's new-found republicanism.

We rebellious subjects are citizens-in-waiting; a gentle, even genteel, polite, civilised but determined vanguard who are fighting a battle centuries after it should have been won. Even so, until perhaps two years ago we were labelled outsiders, mavericks, and loony lefties. We were considered marginal, even by those who should have been our friends, like the scoffers in Charter 88 who contend that we're a diversion from the real battle. In fact, they should realise that we have a common cause: our success will be theirs. Anyway, isn't it us who are making the running at the moment?

In my 32 years as a journalist I can't recall a time when the press has been so openly anti-monarchist. It's unprecedented. *The Economist*, the prestigious *Economist*, generally considered the world's most influential weekly, the paper once edited by that arch-monarchist Walter Bagehot, was the first to declare itself in favour of a republic. Then, a couple of months back, the *Independent on Sunday* not only came out in favour of a republic but has been campaigning vigorously for one in succeeding weeks.

The Guardian and the *Observer* have also both shown republican sympathies. And I don't think yesterday's change of editor at the *Observer* will be any more comforting for the royalist cause. The new editor, Will Hutton, has a chapter in his much-praised book entitled *The Republican Opportunity* in which he argues for the stripping of the Crown's prerogative powers and the end of the hereditary principle. But Will, writing at the beginning of last year, shies away from abolition on the rather feeble grounds that the British would be 'likely...to want to retain the monarch as titular head of state'. Events have moved faster on this

front than the far-sighted new *Observer* editor anticipated.

But forget the republican-minded broadsheets for a moment. I take greater heart from what's been published recently in a tabloid paper that has long trumpeted its loyalty to the Crown: none other than Britain's largest-selling and most controversial daily. Yes, *The Sun* . . .

A couple of weeks ago *The Sun* published the most remarkable set of polls over a five-day period. They were remarkable in two ways: firstly, in the paper even deciding to publish the questions; and secondly, in their subsequent results. The first one asked: Is Prince Charles fit to be King?

The result: 33,226 said No and only 8,878 said Yes. The third one asked: Should the Queen be our last monarch? Yes, replied 5,466. No, said 3,555. I was amazed at this result. But would the editor, Stuart Higgins, dare to ask the next logical question? He didn't disappoint. His fifth poll question asked: Do you

want Charles crowned or a Republic? Charles scored 3,436 but the Republic attracted support from 5,494.

I can't imagine those kinds of questions being published in a popular paper five years ago. The editor would have been fielding calls from outraged readers. It's highly likely the paper would have been boycotted. But republicanism is on the public agenda now. It's not only fashionable for people to think it, it's fashionable for them to talk about it and it's also becoming fashionable for them to contemplate the alternative.

On the other hand, even though *The Sun's* poll results are interesting, mighty interesting, I readily concede that they're flawed. They were telephone polls. They were self-selecting. The questions were loaded. And there was no statistical balance.

Proper pollsters – you know, the ones who always manage to correctly predict the general election result (hush my mouth) – anyway, proper

pollsters pour scorn on the kind of exercise carried out by *The Sun*. And, traditionally, they also have maintained that republicanism is a dead duck. But MORI, which recently carried out a special sampling about the monarchy for the *Independent on Sunday*, came up with some very surprising results indeed. Results so surprising that MORI's chairman, Bob Worcester, told this month's Common Sense dining club meeting they showed 'an unprecedented movement of public opinion'.

I'll just give you – or remind you – of the bull points: For the first time, a majority of the British public think Britain won't have a monarchy in 50 years' time. Only a third of the country, 33%, believe the monarchy has a long-term future while 43% believe it doesn't. To put that in perspective, just six years ago the figures were 69% to 11%. By any standards that's an astonishing transformation in opinion.

A decade ago, by a factor of 15 to 1, an overwhelming proportion of people thought Britain would be worse off without a monarchy. Now it's fallen to just two to one. Another astounding conversion. By the way, this survey was carried out in February so it's probably even stevens by now. Indeed, among young people, those aged 18 to 24, there's already a majority who believe we'd be better off without the House of Windsor. Not that many care: 56% are indifferent. The same movement of opinion is happening over the constitutional role of the monarchy. In 1987, when MORI asked people whether they thought that Britain would be less stable politically without the monarchy, a majority of more than two to one, 59% to 26%, thought it would be less stable. Now these figures, at 43% to 43%, are even.

I could quote many more examples. But here's one final, and given the recent shenanigans at Buckingham Palace, totally unremarkable set of poll findings: there have been precipitous falls in the image of the royal family in the past five years. Are royals important to Britain's image? Down 25 points. Are they hard working? Down 20 points. Are they extravagant? A leap from 16% to 35%. Are they irresponsible? Up from 2% to 20%.

Now these results supposedly represent us with a paradox which runs something like this: we're here today as members of Republic for precisely the opposite reasons that people in this country are beginning to turn their backs on the Crown. It's assumed that our opposition to monarchy is based on principled objections while the people out there, the public, the masses, otherwise known as *Sun* and *Mirror* readers, are opposing monarchy for unprincipled reasons.

Only a third of the country, 33%, believe the monarchy has a long-term future while 43% believe it doesn't. To put that in perspective, just six years ago the figures were 69% to 11%

I admit it: I've fallen into this trap too but I've come to believe that it's not only a patronising standpoint, it's arrant foolishness. History doesn't progress in a logical sequence with every human actor at the same level of understanding. Anyway, there's more than one reason for opposing the monarchy and what the hell's wrong with being against having a royal family if that family is behaving badly? You can always ask other, deeper questions about their very existence later. The important point for us is, no matter the reason why, millions in Britain are now questioning the very existence of the monarchy.

I think one of the reasons I deluded myself, and others, about this so-called split between The Family and The Monarchy is because I allowed myself to pay too much attention to apologists for the monarchy, apologists like the *Daily Telegraph*'s editor, Charles Moore. He consistently asserts that we should differentiate between the Crown and the people who happen to wear it. For a moment it seems like a seductive argument.

Indeed, it's not only an argument. History shows us that the monarchy has indeed been able to reproduce itself. Whenever a family didn't suit, sometimes whenever a family name didn't suit – remember those Battenbergs? – then the family, or its name, has vanished. But another has sprung up in its place to continue the wonderful institution of monarchy.

In other words, according to Moore and his ilk, there is a mysterious, mystical, metaphysical thing called the monarchy which exists independently of those who assume its earthly form. The family are relatively unimportant, pawns in ermine who can be sacrificed at will. The monarchy, however, is sacrosanct.

Now think for a minute and see where that analogy take us. It's a completely false distinction, designed to divert attention from reality. It's a bit like saying there's some metaphysical thing called Crime which is separate from its awful human practitioners, those terrible people called criminals.

Moore cannot bring himself to defend the practice of the people who call themselves Windsors and who happen to have been handed the Crown. So, by smuggling human beings out of the equation, he is able to claim the spiritual purity of the monarchy itself.

To his mind, and that of all who push this spurious argument, the monarchy is greater not only than all of us subjects here today – well, traitor subjects in this room, of course – but it's so essential to the nation of Britain that it exists independently even of those poor downtrodden beings who are the prisoners of its palaces.

I'm afraid this really won't do. The light has been let in on the magic. The people now see the royal family as they see themselves: flawed human beings. The royals aren't special after all. Once they've seen that, then it's only a small step before people ask themselves whether the institution itself, monarchy, is either special or necessary. And that's where Republic comes in.

It is for us to show just why monarchy is unnecessary to the mass of the people but very necessary indeed to Parliament. It is for us to show how the crown prerogative provides prime ministers with immense powers of patronage. It is for us to show how the monarchy cements in place an establishment which reproduces itself generation after generation. It is for us to calm the fears of people who think a republic is some kind of communist conspiracy.

Through a media which, as I've shown, is becoming more and more supportive we must carry these arguments to the people with more clarity and energy than we've ever shown before. Though we're having a good press right now we can't afford to sit back and watch this aristocratic state dismantle itself. We must maintain the pressure at all costs. And that means taking up every argument in that portion of the royalist press which loves to take tea with the Queen at Buckingham Palace garden parties.

But we can't do any of that successfully if we stay aloof from the current rows raging about the royal family. We have to be prepared to make the links between the undemocratic nature of the monarchical system and the undemocratic behaviour of the family.

At our fringe meeting at last year's Labour Party conference I said that the reason I'm a republican had nothing to do with whether or not I liked the royal family. I said I shared Tony Benn's dislike of personalising what is essentially an argument about the mechanics of our constitution and the way in which the monarchy – as an institution – not a group of people acts as a barrier to a properly democratic state.

But I just couldn't help myself. A couple of weeks before the conference I'd read a book which had been smuggled into Britain: *The Housekeeper's Diary* by Wendy Berry. She was housekeeper to the Prince and Princess of Wales from 1985 until 1992. Her book was published in America early last year, but it can't be sold here. Prince Charles's lawyers went to extraordinary lengths to try to stop publication. But under

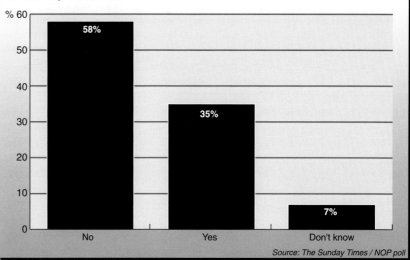

Do you think the monarchy will exist in its present form in 30 years' time?

NOP interviewed 1,073 adults, face to face, at 52 sampling points across Britain on 12th September 1997

Source: The Sunday Times / NOP poll

America's written constitution – a constitution which guarantees freedom of speech – she was able to tell her story.

The people now see the royal family as they see themselves: flawed human beings. The royals aren't special after all

---

It wasn't the details about the disintegrating marriage which fascinated me. What was so revealing was the kind of life enjoyed by not only the royal family, but its various hangers-on. Just a few examples . . . Wendy's son, James – who was a footman at Buckingham Palace – told his mother about his first evening.

James says: 'To be quite frank my initial reaction was total shock . . . What was remarkable was the number of staff – the footmen, butler, Queen's page, cooks, pastry chefs and cellar staff waiting on the royal family's every whim . . . I was flabbergasted by all the staff required to serve four people. The pastry chefs were on hand, for example, because one of the group had mentioned they wanted some bread and butter pudding for dessert. All the kitchen staff naturally stayed on duty to make sure this was produced at the right time at exactly the right temperature.

It was an eye-opener, and there was one maxim I would never forget: four staff can always do a job better than one.'

You won't be surprised that James also said: 'It was a scene which stirred hitherto unrecognised republican thoughts in my brain.' Although we want to remain above the matter of intrusion into marital dramas, it's surely legitimate to enquire into the lifestyle enjoyed by the royal family. Because that lifestyle is totally at odds with the experiences of almost everyone else. It's the most blatant example of privilege. The kind of privilege which is a complete anachronism in a genuine democracy. A privilege of birthright. A privilege open to no other group in our society.

And that's the point, isn't it, of all that I've said this afternoon? James Berry was stirred to republicanism not out of concern about Britain having no written constitution, not because of the abuse of power latent in the crown prerogative, not because royalty cements in place an anachronistic class structure, but out of amazement at the trappings of wealth and privilege.

Our task in the coming year is to pick up arguments like this, to tap into the well of outrage at the antics of a dysfunctional family, to appreciate the growing concerns of people who don't want a monarch but are scared of what might replace it.

© *Roy Greenslade / Republic, 1996*

Watchdogs to scrutinise royal finances

Details of how the Queen spends taxpayers' money are to be scrutinised by government spending watchdogs after MPs criticised the Royal Household's lack of accountability. Fran Abrams, Political Correspondent, examines the outcome of an inquiry which has taken five years to complete.

An announcement is expected by mid-February on how the books will be opened up after a critical report yesterday from the Commons' Public Accounts Committee.

While the Queen's personal finances will remain private, the Treasury will give the National Audit Office access to details of how she spends public money. The Royal Family receives £42.3m from the Government each year, about £20m of which goes on accommodation for staff, pensioners and others.

Occupants of the 265 apartments and houses could never afford market rents on them, the committee said in its report, based on evidence given in 1995. On average, they paid £45 per week, which would increase to £83 per week as planned reforms were introduced. But royal properties let out commercially would fetch between £150 and £850 per week.

The Royal Household charges just £9,000 per year in rent for seven properties in Windsor worth £850,000 – just over 1 per cent of capital value and about a tenth of the market rent.

The report expressed concern about the size and salary of the Royal Household. Although a new system had been introduced under which there would be a deduction from salaries to cover the cost of accommodation, it would take a long time before the full benefits were achieved. The system had not yet been extended to senior staff and the progress in applying the contracts to all staff should be monitored.

The committee's chairman, David Davis, also said it seemed that the new system would subsidise the Civil List rather than reduce the cost of palaces.

There was also anger that £900,000 was spent refurbishing accommodation for two senior officials. The outlay was necessary because it had previously been left empty for more than a decade and had not been touched since its previous occupant arrived in 1923.

'We are concerned that part of the estate was neglected in this way,' the report said.

The Royal Household said the cost would be recouped through rent in 20 years, while in fact it would take 30 years.

The report said royal officials claimed wrongly that furnishings which cost £310,000 were needed because staff had to hold official functions at home. Later they admitted 'there was not a huge amount of official entertaining and the accommodation was not really provided for that purpose'.

Plans to reduce the number of properties to 205 came as a 'surprise' to the committee, which had not been told. 'We are therefore concerned that the substantial scope for releasing accommodation was not brought to the committee's attention,' it said.

Mr Davis said the Royal Household had taken the issues seriously, adding: 'Some of the detail in our report might now be dated but the access issues remain unresolved.'

A spokesman for Buckingham Palace said Parliament already had scrutiny of the Queen's accounts through figures given to the Department of Culture, Media and Sport. 'There is currently no direct access to accounts because the Queen is accountable to Parliament through her ministers and the money is granted to government departments and not the Royal Household.'

© The Independent December, 1997

Don't ask the Queen to change

A surprising view from left-wing historian, Ben Pimlott, Professor of Politics and Contemporary History, Birkbeck College, London

Does Britain want a bicycling monarchy, a youth culture monarchy, a touchy-freely monarchy, or no monarchy at all?

Questions that have been knocked about since the Queen's *annus horribilis* speech in 1992 have suddenly become urgent. Reform of the monarchy is on everybody's agenda. Yet after five years of putting it on the backburner, exactly what the British people want remains a mystery.

When Earl Spencer pledged his 'blood family' to help his nephews avoid the danger of immersion in duty and tradition, we felt we knew what he meant. Rival images entered our heads – Royals in tweeds and tartan versus Royals in jeans.

But if almost everybody seemed to know which they preferred, it remains harder to work out a more solid manifesto for change.

Should the Queen get less public money? Should she have fewer residences, and no yacht? Should she turn up at the state opening of Parliament in a cocktail dress? Should the minor Royals be pensioned off, more than they have been already?

The message from the part-angry, part-respectful crowds of mourners – as from Diana's brother – had little to do with these questions. Nor was there any hint of opposition to the monarchy as such. Instead, it was about style – of which the dead Princess was ever the uncrowned queen in everything she did.

People loved Diana not because she had a high sense of duty but because she seemed the most accessible member of the Royal Family. Unlike the other Royals, she did not wear a mask. In word, gesture and facial expression, she was the easiest to imagine as a friend.

She shared the public's tastes, hang-ups and sense of humour, and wore the clothes the woman in the street would have liked to wear, if she'd had the money. Above all, she seemed to need the public as much as they needed her.

When she died, they wanted to be comforted by those who remained, as she would have comforted them. Hence the demand for public symbols of grief.

For the Queen to be bounced by recent events into a campaign of baby-kissing would simply make the public cringe

---

If anger seemed to rise against the Royal Family last week, it was partly because of the absence of an equivalent shoulder to weep on, itself a reminder of what had been lost.

Here is the core of the problem. What the public wants, more than a reformed monarchy, is a substitute for Diana.

To meet its critics, the Royal Family can cut down on the ceremonial the public usually loves, or accept more, fewer or different engagements. What it cannot do is transform the character and the personality of those who are its members into Diana seem-alikes.

For the Queen to be bounced by recent events into a campaign of baby-kissing would simply make the public cringe. It may be that William and Harry will have different instincts, but we will have to wait and see. However, to train or cajole them into an emulation of their mother would be to do precisely what Earl Spencer pledged himself against.

Should the older Royals show more 'compassion' – a word linked by the Prime Minister, and others, specifically to the Princess?

Arguably, compassion can take different forms. The Queen as patron of many charities and as Head of the Commonwealth, Princess Anne as an active President of the Save the Children Fund, and Charles with his portfolio of trusts and schemes, have scarcely been less involved in the compassion business than Diana.

Nor have they shied away from controversy in the pursuit of their campaigns.

Charles's outspokenness has got him into trouble, while the new

I SUPPOSE IT HAD TO COME – A BICYCLE MONARCHY!

KenPyne

South Africa gratefully remembers the key role the Queen played, sometimes to the irritation of her government, as an opponent of apartheid.

Should they, like Diana, use the media to communicate their innermost feelings? 'Stuffy' and 'hidebound' are terms used to describe the older Royals. Ought they to respond to criticism by making themselves more available as flesh-and-blood human beings, through television for example?

One answer is that they already have, with disastrous consequences. Some maintain that the monarchy's problems date from 1969, when BBC cameras were let into Buckingham Palace for a revolutionary film called *Royal Family*.

Overnight, the Royals ceased to be two-dimensional figureheads, and became quirky players in a national soap. Respect declined and irritation increased.

The worm turned with *It's A Royal Knockout* in 1987, a charity show designed by Prince Edward (and wisely avoided by the Prince and Princess of Wales) to show the younger Royals as ordinary people, having normal fun; but which seemed to reveal them, instead, as a collection of buffoons.

The lowest point came seven years later when Prince Charles confessed adultery to an audience of millions. According to this view, if the Queen and her mother only have retained something of the mystery on which the monarchy depends, it is because of their restraint.

Arguably, too, proposals which require the Royals to behave in ways that do not come easily to them miss the point of the monarchy. An institution that follows strict rules of heredity cannot be expected to behave like a political party.

If you have a Royal Family, you have to make the best of whatever personalities the genetic lottery comes up with. Short of criminality or the break of fundamental rules, you are stuck with them and their limitations for as long as they live.

To survive, the monarchy must evolve, as it always has done in the past, inventing new traditions and adopting new practices. Charles

---

Ought they to respond to criticism by making themselves more available as flesh-and-blood human beings, through television for example?

---

should ensure that his children are equipped for professions that amount to more than being mannequins for service uniforms.

He needs to see that they meet ordinary children of their own age, not just boys who go to Eton. The Queen needs to invite more people, more often, into the royal residences. Meanwhile, some of the crustier aspects of monarchy – knighthoods of the Garter given to royal cronies, for instance – should go.

The Prime Minister will have such changes in mind as he continues to talk to the Queen. What he cannot be expected to say is: 'Ma'am, adopt a different personality like a new set of clothes.'

After 45 years of mainly impeccable service on the throne, that is not something that can be expected of her.

• Ben Pimlott is author of *The Queen: A Biography Of Elizabeth II*.

© *The Daily Mail*
September, 1997

The British Royal Family

- Half the British public expect the monarchy to disappear within fifty years
- But six in ten say Britain still needs one
- Over half say they have less respect for the Royal Family than ten years ago
- Only four in ten think Prince Charles will make a good king

Over the past six years there has been a significant increase in the proportion of people who think Britain will no longer have a monarchy in the future. While just one in five think Britain will not have a monarchy in ten years, as many think Britain will not have one in fifty years – a rise of 37 points since 1990. However, six in ten disagree with the statement that Britain no longer needs a monarchy.

Over a third of people think Prince Charles will make a bad king when he comes to the throne, a rise of 31 points since 1991. Similarly, over one in two Britons say that they have less respect for the Royal Family now then ten years ago. Two in five blame the Duchess of York for having done the most damage to the Royal Family's reputation, while a third blame Prince Charles.

Not only has increasing criticism been directed at individuals, over the past few years there has been a shift in the public's perception of the Royal Family in general. In particular, since 1990 the proportion of people describing them as extravagant has risen by 18 points while just 8% say they have high moral standards, compared with 29% in 1990. In addition, fewer describe them as being respected or in touch with ordinary people.

The issue of how the Royal Family is financed is salient to the majority to people, with nearly eight in ten saying that it should pay its own way. One in two do not think that Britain gets good value from the money it spends on the Royal Family.

When asked what things the Royal Family does that are useful, charity work is mentioned most frequently closely followed by its role as ambassadors for the country. Nearly a quarter of the public cannot think of anything.

© *MORI*
January, 1997

Off with their heads

Republicanism and opposition to monarchy in England has a long history

Kings and queens represent a hangover from the Middle Ages. The powers they have inherited allow them to side with the most reactionary elements in society in order to block all progress.

This was the thinking behind the most famous, and to date decisive, move against the monarchy: the English Revolution of 1649-49. The revolution came to a head-on collision with the swaggering, boastful and despotic Charles I.

The revolution first tried to compromise with Charles, but to enjoy success it had to get to grips with the King and his power. Oliver Cromwell told his troops:

'I will not deceive you nor make you believe, as my commission has it, that you are going to fight for the King and Parliament: if the King were before me I would shoot him as another, if your conscience will not allow you to do as much, go and serve elsewhere.'

Cromwell was as good as his word. He led the side that wanted Charles executed and the monarchy gone with him.

To those who sought compromise, Cromwell was clear: 'We will cut off his head with the crown upon it.'

On 30 January 1648 Charles was executed as a 'tyrant, traitor, murderer and enemy to the country'. That should have been that. However, the revolution had been made by all sorts of different groups in society. The emerging capitalist class wanted to get rid of the old feudal trappings and restrictions on trade, but did not want to challenge the rights of property. Many of the poorer people, who were usually very enthusiastic for the revolution, drew the conclusion that if power could no longer be inherited why should wealth?

They were crushed by the army generals. The men of property – fearing further social change – were happy to restore the monarchy in 1660.

The Glorious Revolution of 1688 – when James II fled and the Dutch King William took the throne – ensured that never again would a king dare to seriously challenge parliament or the immensely powerful capitalist class.

The second great wave of republican sentiment was precipitated by the American Revolution of 1776. Those initially leading it groped slowly towards the need to sever all links with George III, the English king. As the King introduced a series of taxes and punitive laws against the colony more and more people asked why had a good system gone bad.

One man though understood that the system itself was at fault. Thomas Paine had moved to America from England in the early days of the revolution, and now became the populiser of republican and independence sentiments. His pamphlet *Common Sense* roared like a hurricane through the absurdities of monarchy. 'Hereditary Monarchy,' he wrote, 'was as absurd as a hereditary wise man, a hereditary mathematician or a hereditary poet laureate.'

Common Sense sold a staggering 150,000 copies, and was second only to the Bible as the most widely bought book. It became a hugely popular pamphlet among the poor in England.

Paine tore apart the notion of the succession. Little wonder he was feared and loathed by the establishment. When he wrote *The Rights of Man* in defence of the French Revolution he struck fear into the hearts of the English ruling class.

Paine was vilified, denounced and eventually had to flee the country. Nevertheless an incredible half million copies were sold. The

masses hated the monarchy, and the movement had to be repressed and physically broken to prevent it spreading. Even so, its ideas remained popular in some circles, for example among the early nineteenth century poets such as Shelley.

But republicanism in the nineteenth century became more and more tied up with the working class movement, as the great division in society developed between those who owned property and those who did not. The Chartist movement contained many prominent republicans. The *Red Republican*, edited by the Chartist Julian Harney, published the writings of Karl Marx and Frederick Engels.

The Chartists' six demands that became known as The People's Charter were accepted with enthusiasm by hundreds of thousands of industrial workers – 200,000 rallied in Glasgow, 80,000 in Newcastle, 250,000 in Leeds and 300,000 in Manchester. Engels declared that the six points were 'sufficient to overthrow the whole constitution, queen and lords included'.

In 1842 the Chartists presented their second petition to the House of Commons attacking the wealth of the royal parasites:

'Your petitioners would direct the attention…to the great disparity existing between wages of the producing millions and the salaries of those whose comparative usefulness ought to be questioned, where riches and luxury prevail amongst the rulers and poverty and starvation amongst the ruled.'

With the defeat of Chartism after 1848, and counter revolution throughout Europe, republicanism became less of an issue. But it resurfaced in the 1860s and 1870s because of the unpopularity of Queen Victoria's rule. In the early 1870s, 84 republican clubs were founded and there were complaints about the money spent on the Queen. More than once the House of Commons debated a motion demanding the diminishing of royal power.

This tradition has been hidden behind decades of jubilees, royal weddings and coronations. But it is one we should claim as our own.

© *Socialist Review*

Should Royals bow to reform?

Sir, The annual spectacle of the State Opening of Parliament is one of which our nation can be justly proud. The symbol of the monarch demonstrating the democratic link between the Crown, Parliament and the people is fundamental to our parliamentary democracy.

I regard any suggestion that the pomp and ceremony of the occasion be watered down in the public interest as misguided, and I believe that the spectacle of our Queen travelling to Parliament in a horse-drawn State Coach rather than a car meets with the overwhelming support of our citizens.

The modernisation programme being undertaken by the inner circle of the Royal Family is starting to reap reward in terms of public opinion. Meanwhile, the State Opening should be retained for generations to come, as a glittering reflection of all that is good about our British constitution.

Yours faithfully,
Mike Howson,
Leek, Staffordshire

Sir, It is very important that reforms to the monarchy are not guided by those who have no liking for the institution in any case. It would be like a Chinese restaurant having its menu subjected to change by people that do not like Chinese food, only to spoil it for those who do.

Yours faithfully,
Martin Graham,
Hollingbourne, Kent

Sir, If the Royal Family is to adapt to public opinion, can we now look to the termination of the unseemly practice of foreign tennis players at Wimbledon having to bow or curtsy to whomever is sitting in the royal box?

Yours faithfully,
James Joss,
Woodbridge, Suffolk

Sir, You report (March 9) that 'By tradition [lord-lieutenants] are retired military officers.' The tradition, for which there was a sound basis, has long since faded.

Of the 56 lord-lieutenants in England and Wales only ten could be described as retired military officers, and even they should not be stereotyped as having an inordinate love of tradition. At least 20 of us are, or have been, businessmen – and there are four female lord-lieutenants.

Yours faithfully,
Hugo Brunner
Lord-Lieutenant of Oxfordshire,
© *Reprinted with the kind permission of the writers and the Times Newspaper Ltd March, 1998*

Letters

Towards a British Republic

Edgar Wilson, editor of Republic's journal, outlines the principled case for a republic and rebuts arguments against it

Conservatives have a blunt old saw that goes 'If it ain't broke – don't fix it.' They believe that the monarchy has served and, more important, can continue to serve the country very well, so it would be folly to change it very much, let alone abolish it altogether. This conviction survives like a palsy only in the brains of those who cannot, or will not, see how the monarchy lurks beneath Britain's chronic economic, social and political problems; legitimates the caste system that stultifies the whole nation; and infantilises the mass of its admirers. The institution of monarchy is broke and needs fixing one way or another.

Incorrigible conservatives will say that change has already been tried, without success. They argue against a British republic saying Britain (really England) has had its experiment with republicanism, under Cromwell, and discovered it didn't work. Only in England, perhaps, would anybody say that because three and a half centuries ago something didn't work then that is the end of the matter for all eternity. Conservatives are great believers in experience and there is no denying that experience is a great teacher. One thing it certainly teaches us is not to rely on the continuation or effectiveness of institutions the only legitimisation for which is that they happen, like slavery and the subordination of women and the British monarchy, to have been around for a very long time. There is no good reason to suppose that England is incapable of republican government, and this is one way to fix the monarchy. I want to suggest that we should have a republic on principle and that we can abolish the monarchy without violating public opinion.

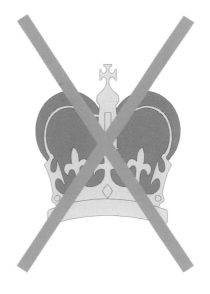

Principled republicanism

It is often observed, even by conservative-minded royalists, that hereditary monarchy is not an institution that would appear on any drawing board if a constitution were to be designed from scratch. Like the Irishman giving directions to Kilkenny, the constitutional draughtsman would advise us not to start from here, where we're at, with a hereditary monarchy if we want to take the road to a rationally defensible constitution for Britain in the twenty-first century. The reasons why this is so are simple and straightforward enough, though they are so seldom made explicit that it is instructive to remind ourselves what they are.

First there is the fundamental moral principle that it is a good thing that people are in charge of their own lives. In practice, this means that they should not be subject to laws and governments which they do not consent to, at least tacitly. Further, in practice this goes with the least bad policy, that of representative democracy, the workable form of popular sov-

ereignty. We can then consider hereditary monarchy against the classic democratic ideals of the French republic and the practical form they typically take.

Hereditary monarchy is incompatible with liberty because, as the great liberal philosopher John Stuart Mill explained, traditional institutions like the monarchy are the chief instruments of repression of the British people because individuals are crushed by the weight of custom. Another great liberal philosopher in our own time, Isaiah Berlin, might have been writing about popular royalism when he explains that: 'The triumph of despotism is to force the slaves to declare themselves to be free. It may need no force: the slaves may proclaim their freedom quite sincerely: but they are none the less slaves.'

Hereditary monarchy is self-evidently incompatible with equality and fraternity. As Peregrine Worsthorne explains: 'The essential function of royalty involves being set apart from and above the rest of mankind.' Significantly, Worsthorne approves of the fact that cabinet ministers in the elected government are obliged to symbolically 'bend the knee' before the hereditary monarch; thus showing how 'the democracy ... approaches the monarchy from a posture of subjection'. As if legitimate democratic government were in need of even symbolic subjection to a hereditary billionaire.

In practice, democracy requires that all public offices, especially the most important ones, are representative and accountable. This in turn, in practice, requires that incumbents should be elected. Needless to say, election to office is not a guarantee of the sagacity, competence and good character of incumbents in office.

But at least the people only have themselves and their compatriots to blame for bad choices, and they can be changed.

Incidentally, it is noteworthy that by the hereditary principle the kind of personal problems and scandals evident in the *annus horribilis* are only to be expected. Even Bagehot, the great defender of constitutional monarchy, recognised that there were 'great dangers' attached to hereditary heads of state if they are ordinary persons of 'restricted experience and common capacity (and we have no right to suppose that by miracle they may be more)'. Bagehot's solution was to keep the monarchy away from daylight. As we have recently learned, this is not an option any more.

Evidently the institution of hereditary monarchy is essentially incompatible with the prevailing defensible principles and practices of popular sovereignty and the democratic institutions that embody them. The republican tradition on the other hand is based on ideals of the autonomy of individual citizens, popular sovereignty and representative government, all of which are compatible with democratic principles and practices.

Only irredeemable English chauvinists will ignore the practical effectiveness of the republican ideals in nations such as the United States and Switzerland or ignore the lessons to be learned. More to the point, there is in Britain, including England, a very strong republican tradition that has been effectively suppressed by establishment monarchism. This is the honourable tradition of John Ball, John Lilbourne, Thomas Paine and Keir Hardy. Significantly, some of the nation's greatest poets, including Milton, Wordsworth, Blake and Shelley, have been republicans. Nothing could be further from the truth than Edmund Burke's claim that republicanism is a philosophy for cold hearts, because the republican ideals of liberty, equality and fraternity are capable of inspiring the most intensely emotional commitments. To the question of popular sentiment we can now turn.

The popularity of the British monarchy

Leaving aside for the sake of argument the recent perturbations, the British monarchy has been thought to be overwhelmingly popular in recent times, and this constitutes the main obstacle to republicanism in Britain, or the most obvious one. Paradoxically, it seems that the democratic principle of majorities supports an institution which is in principle essentially undemocratic. The facts seem plain enough. Until recently, about 1986, 85% of people expressed a preference for monarchy and only 15% positively preferred a republic. One view of these opinion poll results is that they are highly suspect, and do not really lend support for the conclusion that the population of Britain overwhelmingly and enthusiastically favours monarchy. Leonard Harris, after a lifetime polling public opinion on the subject, thought that most British people tend to accept the monarchy like the weather. That is to say, they accept it because it is there and there's nothing you can do about it, no matter how horrible it is or what you really think about it.

There are two sorts of explanation for the prevalence of expressed support for the monarchy in Britain since the Second World War. More recent events happen to provide a convenient test that enables us to choose between them. The first explanation for popular royalism is that the monarchy is deeply rooted in the British psyche. This view was first advanced in the 1930s by Freud's biographer, Ernest Jones. It was taken up by Kingsley Martin in the 1960s and has been elaborated on recently by Tom Nairn, most notably in his

---

There is no earthy reason in principle why in a supposed democracy we should have a constitutional monarchy

---

impressive book *The enchanted glass: Britain and its monarchy* (1988). According to this view not only is people's idea of their country linked essentially to the monarchy, but the very idea of who they are themselves is deeply rooted unconsciously in some conception of Britishness as royalist. It is not possible, neither is it necessary, to elaborate this view here. It is sufficient to note some significant implications of it. If monarchy is really deeply rooted in the British psyche as the hypothesis suggests, then people will tend strongly to be immune to bald facts and rational arguments which count against their beliefs and feelings, or in favour of alternatives. Further implications are that it will be a waste of time to advance evidence and argument against the monarchy, and political suicide for any political party seeking popular support openly to attack the deeply cherished institution. This, certainly, has been the attitude towards popular royalism found among most sceptics, especially politicians.

There is an alternative view of popular royalism that can be derived from some reflection on opinion polls and what we know generally about the British way of life and the British people. In this view, support for the monarchy is relatively shallow where it exists, is less widespread than is commonly supposed, and is anyway the artificial product of public relations, propaganda and indoctrination. Added to this is the effective suppression of criticism and the dissemination of fair accounts of practical alternatives.

Significantly, the distinguished and honourable republican tradition is effectively excluded not only from the general culture in Britain, but even from the advanced curriculum for Politics and Government in schools. Thomas Paine, who is well known as the 'greatest Englishman' to students of the republics of the United States and France, is unknown in his own country. His democratic republican writings are still proscribed reading in Northern Irish jails. If this view is correct then people will be amenable to criticism of the monarchy and will readily change their opinion about it when presented with facts and arguments that count against it.

Conclusion

There is no earthly reason in principle why in a supposed democracy we should have a constitutional monarchy; on the contrary, there are the very best of reasons of principle why we should have what is incompatible with it, that is a republic. Also, the main obstacle to a republic in practice, the popularity of the monarchy, is a shallow thing which can be dissipated by counter-propaganda that favours an eminently justifiable alternative. These conclusions may serve as benchmarks for practical reformers who seek to remedy the universally recognised malaise of British public life. The Australians have already decided to do it.

No republican can seriously suppose that abolition or very radical reform of the monarchy would in itself remedy all of Britain's problems. Nevertheless, radical change along these lines is undoubtedly a necessary if not a sufficient condition for desperately needed improvement in the state of our nation.

*© Republic
January, 1998*

Actually, the people these few weeks have been bad for are the republicans

By Peregrine Worsthorne

It was boredom that finally drove the French people to do away with their monarchy in 1848, and whatever the British people may feel about the monarchy in 1997, it is certainly not boredom. The story of that last king is worth recalling. Rather than calling himself 'King of France', he called himself 'King of the French' – i.e. the people's king. Rather than dressing himself up in brocaded uniform, he dressed down in the clothes of the man of the street. Rather than surrounding himself with *ancien régime* noblemen, he surrounded himself with members of the new bourgeoisie. It didn't work. The people grew bored and sent him packing, and then took the first opportunity to opt again for a further period of Napoleonic drama and excitement.

Drama and excitement, however, are precisely what our royal family does provide, to a quite extraordinary degree, and not only for the British but, it would seem, for the entire human race. Far from boring the people, the monarchy clearly fascinates the people, obsesses the people. Even female columnists who claim to be 'indifferent' write about little else. Those who solemnly proclaim that the monarchy is irrelevant to the modern world, therefore, are plainly wrong. It is

essentially relevant. Nothing about Britain today is more relevant. In the monarchy we have a unique asset. So far as the rest of the world is concerned, it is the most important thing about us.

If anything, it seems to me, the tragic death of Diana, Princess of Wales, confirms rather than contradicts this truth. What would the human race do without the house of Windsor? Its births, deaths and marriages have become an important part of everyone's life, and, in the same way that even the most anticlerical Italian has to recognise that it is the papacy that puts Italy on the map, so must even the most

> *Today it makes no more sense to talk of abolishing the monarchy than it does to talk of abolishing Shakespeare*

republican Englishman recognise that it is the monarchy which puts Britain on the map. Would it be too much to say that the British monarchy, like the papacy, has become a universal institution? I don't think so. Both, in their different ways, help to bring light into the world, and never has this universalist side of the monarchy been seen to such good effect as during the last few weeks. How this has happened is difficult to say, but it has happened and today it makes no more sense to talk of abolishing the monarchy than it does to talk of abolishing Shakespeare.

That should be the starting-point of any serious discussion about the monarchy, but it does not seem to be. Since coming back from holiday last week, I have been invited to take part in two television programmes asking the question, 'Has the monarchy a future?' as if the answer was in doubt. The Queen's ambivalent reaction to the Diana tragedy, it was said, showed that she was out of touch with the modern age, just as Prince Charles's male chauvinist attitude to his wife showed him to be antediluvian. But surely what these criticisms showed was a widespread desire not to get rid of the monarchy but to modernise it. If the public, sensing the Queen's

20

ambivalence about her daughter-in-law, had expressed their disapproval of this lukewarm attitude by asking her to stay away from the funeral, that would indeed have been worrying. But of course they did exactly the opposite. Her participation was felt to be essential. For the people to mourn was not enough. For the mourning to be complete the Sovereign had to take the lead. Only with her active participation could the catharsis be complete.

In other words, this so-called anger against the Queen took the form of wanting more of her rather than wanting less; of expressing love, albeit frustrated love, rather than indifference. Heaven knows, the popular demands were scarcely radical, let alone revolutionary: that the Union Jack should fly at half mast and that the Queen should come out of the palace before the funeral to share the grief of the crowds. If this is republicanism, then Tom Paine might as well never have uttered. That there is a demand for monarchical modernisation is certainly the case, but the last thing true republicans have ever wanted is modernisation, because modernisation spells prolongation.

A lot of defeatist nonsense has been written on the subject of modernisation, quite a bit by me. Strip away the pomp and pageantry, protocol and ceremonial, and nothing much would be left. The yawning gap between the royals and the people could not be narrowed without putting majesty at risk. That has been my drift. But the Princess has shown this to be untrue. Yes, she was very much a people's princess, as Mr Blair called her, but the emphasis should be put quite as much on the noun as on the adjective. Most of the pictures of her on the Kensington Palace railings, I noticed, had her wearing a tiara – every inch a princess. In the old days when monarchs ruled they had to overawe. That the people should fear them was far more important than that they should love them. Hence the protocol about royals always being portrayed as stern and formal, usually on horseback, and never smiling and friendly. Now that monarchs only reign rather than rule, however,

much of the ceremony and protocol designed to maintain distance – with a view to overawing – can safely be dispensed with. The Princess proved that and it is a lesson which I do not doubt the royal family has taken very much to heart.

Great constitutional changes are afoot and they will certainly include the monarchy. But my guess is that Mr Blair will include the monarchy – particularly Prince Charles – as a partner rather than a target

---

Not that they had not begun to do so before. When I was young the most characteristic shot of a royal was inspecting a military guard of honour. In recent years it has increasingly become attending charitable functions. Long before the Princess came on the scene Prince Charles took the lead in this respect. Also, unlike the Duke of Edinburgh, who in his heyday was most characteristically photographed in uniform, the son is most characteristically portrayed in mufti.

Clearly more softening up will have to be done before the monarchy catches up with the new age but, with Mr Blair in charge, this should present no difficulty.

Here the monarchy is very fortunate. Just as Mr Disraeli proved the ideal prime minister to give Queen Victoria a triumphant new lease of life towards the end of her reign, Mr Blair looks like being the ideal prime minister to do the same for our present Queen. Whether he meant to undertake this task is difficult to say. But having won such great popular acclaim for his statesmanship in steering the royal family through the Diana drama, he is unlikely not to wish to continue to play this Disraelian – not to mention Baldwinian – role which has already served him so well. New Labour – new monarchy. Of all the strange and surprising things to flow from the Princess's tragic death, that partnership may prove to be the most historic.

All's well that ends well. Great constitutional changes are afoot and they will certainly include the monarchy. But my guess is that Mr Blair will include the monarchy – particularly Prince Charles – as a partner rather than a target. Pity the republicans. It is for them that the bells are truly tolling.

© *The Spectator*
September, 1997

Who would you like to see succeed the Queen?

NOP interviewed 1,073 adults, face to face, at 52 sampling points across Britain on 12th September 1997

- Prince William: 60%
- Prince Charles: 31%
- Others / Don't know: 9%

Source: The Sunday Times / NOP poll

House of Windsor split over new look

By Kim Sengupta

Plans to reform the Royal Family led to claims yesterday that Prince Philip is obstructing change, and counterclaims that MPs leaked details of the plan prematurely and embarrassed Buckingham Palace.

Several newspapers yesterday said the Duke of Edinburgh and the Prince of Wales are said to be on opposing sides on the reforms, with the Queen steering a delicate course, although she is aware of the public mood for change since the death of Diana, Princess of Wales.

Prince Philip is known to have the support of the Queen Mother in his opposition to the proposals, which include the abolition of bowing and curtsying and the restriction of the title 'Royal Highness'. He is said to have strongly expressed his disapproval to Prince Charles's office and to Buckingham Palace officials.

Tony Blair is considering reforms to the House of Lords which could see Prince Charles and the Dukes of Gloucester and York lose their seats in the upper house.

Prince Philip's view is that the reforms of the Sixties and Seventies have not benefited the family, and going further down that path would weaken the monarchy. He is also believed to resent the perception that change is being driven by the death of the Princess of Wales.

The reform package was discussed by the Way Ahead group of Royal advisers presided over by the Queen and attended by the Duke of Edinburgh, the Prince of Wales, the Duke of York and the Princess Royal. There was said to be annoyance at the Palace that the details were then leaked to the press.

Some courtiers believe that Mr Blair's government is trying to bounce the Royal Family into carrying out sweeping reforms, and the leak was designed to create a *fait accompli*.

One source said: 'This is not the first time this has happened. There has been a series of timed leaks, and discussion documents presented as facts. One has got to ask, who is driving the agenda and why?'

The Buckingham Palace website was visited 100 million times in its first year, making it one of the most popular Internet sites in the world

The Prime Minister and the majority of the Labour Party are known strongly to favour the reforms. Downing Street has denied responsibility for the leaks.

Fresh evidence of the Government's desire for change came with reports that the Palace is being pressed to simplify the State Opening of Parliament by doing away with some of the traditional pomp.

Plans to reform the House of Lords, where the Queen makes her annual speech to parliament, will now move ahead without further consultation with the Opposition. Mr Blair is said to be angry at the leaking of contacts with the Conservatives on the reform package.

Moves to take the title of HRH away from the Duke of York's two daughters, Princesses Beatrice and Eugenie, was another issue causing problems.

The Labour MP Alan Williams, a senior member of the Commons Public Accounts Committee, and a long-term critic of royal expenditure, said this might not be 'the cleverest move, because some might interpret it, wrongly, as vindictive. I don't think it matters as far as the public are concerned.' Mr Williams added that the rest of the reform proposals were merely cosmetic and a 'PR exercise'.

The Buckingham Palace website was visited 100 million times in its first year, making it one of the most popular Internet sites in the world.

© *The Independent*
March, 1998

Ken Pyne

The Queen torn over reforms

Philip battles bid by princes to modernise Royals.
By Joe Murphy, Political Editor

The Queen is caught in the middle of a crucial argument between her husband and her sons over the modernisation of the Royal Family.

She finds herself locked in one of the most difficult personal crises of her 46-year reign over reforms which have split her family and advisers.

On one side, she is being advised by her deeply conservative husband, Prince Philip, that Britain's first family is too ancient and steeped in history to be changed.

But the Queen is also under heavy pressure from Prince Charles and Prince Andrew to speed up the pace of reform to safeguard the Throne by keeping it in step with public opinion.

The conflict brings to a head a year of bitter in-fighting between the Palace old guard and reformers, who believe the death of Princess Diana has accelerated the need for change.

Details of the family split emerged, *The Mail on Sunday* can disclose, after a recent meeting of the Way Ahead group at which the strategy for the future was vigorously debated.

One senior source said: 'The Queen is in a very difficult and unenviable position. She is torn between two conflicting views from those closest to her.' At stake is a raft of dramatic reforms which would have been unthinkable only a few years ago. They include a radical suggestion that the title 'Royal Highness' – now held by 18 family members – should be restricted to the heir to the throne and his (or her) immediate successor.

If applied now, it would mean that Prince William would be known as His Royal Highness but his brother, Prince Harry, would not.

And some factions in the deeply divided household want the Queen to begin the process by removing the title from many now holding it, including the Princesses Beatrice and Eugenie, the daughters of Prince Andrew and the Duchess of York.

Prince Philip has emerged as an implacable opponent of all suggestions being debated. A towering patriarchal figure at the Palace, he has always been deferred to by the Queen on most matters affecting the immediate Royal Family.

At their Golden Wedding celebrations only last November, she publicly acknowledged him as 'my strength and stay all these years'. And she added: 'I and his whole family owe him a debt greater than he will ever claim or we shall ever know.'

While in public, his duty has always meant him being one pace behind the Queen, in family matters he has taken the lead.

His attitude to both the Princess of Wales and the Duchess of York when their marriages went wrong was uncompromising.

And he is adamant now that further public pressure to reform the monarchy should be resisted.

The source said last night: 'He feels the family has done enough, particularly after deciding to pay income tax and cut the Civil List.'

Philip is believed to be backed by the Queen Mother and the Princess Royal, although Anne is said to be torn between her father and the advice of her husband, Commander Tim Laurence, an advocate of change.

Prince Charles is, on balance, a moderniser but continues to agonise over the issue. He sees the need to reform but can also understand the importance of maintaining Royal Family traditions. He worries that the public has not recognised the considerable changes the Palace has already made. But his brother Prince Andrew is emerging as a keen exponent of reform and, to many people's surprise, is becoming an influential figure. He may well hold the key to the success of the modernisation argument.

If he agrees – as seems possible – that his daughters should relinquish their HRH titles, it would make it very difficult for others further down the Royal pecking order to hang on to theirs.

Friends of Andrew's divorced wife, Sarah, say she will agree to his wishes and would not resist any change to Beatrice and Eugenie's status – as long as the children are not singled out and other minor Royals are dealt with in a fair package of reform.

The Queen's youngest son, Prince Edward, also supports slimming down the Royal Family.

And the proposals will put pressure on minor Royals, such as the Duke and Duchess of Kent, the Duke and Duchess of Gloucester and Prince and Princess Michael of Kent, to give up their HRH titles.

This 'decommissioning' would save millions of pounds of taxpayers' money in security and the cost of providing them with Royal flights and other privileges. They would become virtually private citizens depending on their own resources.

Their tenure of apartments in Kensington Palace is being looked at, too.

Buckingham Palace has continued to deny that existing holders would be 'stripped' of the HRH title. But last night the matter was unresolved. © *The Mail on Sunday March, 1998*

Soames hails Royal Family's staying power

Let them make changes they think fit, he says. By Alice Thomson and Rachel Sylvester

The British monarchy has been around for 1,000 years and is not finished yet, according to Nicholas Soames, the former defence minister and equerry to the Prince of Wales.

'An organisation needs to evolve or it will die,' he said. 'But it looks like the Royal Family are being pushed into it. We're all going to be cast in the Labour Party style.'

Mr Soames, who has known the Prince of Wales since he was seven, stressed that his views were his own and he had not been asked to speak out by the Prince. But his concerns are shared by many in the Royal circle who fear that the constitution will be undermined by hasty reform.

He said members of the Royal Family were already thinking hard about how they should modernise their way of life and institutions.

The Way Ahead group, set up to discuss reform, which includes members of the family and senior palace officials, has an 'incredibly difficult job ahead' and the members should not be put under pressure from outside.

'The Royal Family has not gone, it is not finished,' he said.

He added: 'I fear the Prime Minister is going to bounce institutions into reform in the name of new Britain. I think they need to be extremely cautious in the advice they offer the Royal Family. It's not a question of no reform and digging one's toes in.

'But I don't see why the Government should bully the Royal Family into reforming into a cool Britannia. It's all nonsense and we shouldn't play the game.'

Mr Soames warned that the Government's pledge to abolish the voting rights of hereditary peers would inevitably 'impact through to the Royal Family'.

Many supporters of the monarchy fear that left-wing Labour backbenchers with republican instincts, who would like to see the Queen replaced with a president, will not be satisfied by reform of the Lords.

He also criticised the leaking of private polls commissioned by the Way Ahead group that showed many people thought the Royal Family was 'out of touch' with ordinary people.

The Queen is said to be resisting attempts by the Government to remove much of the pomp and ceremony surrounding the annual State Opening of Parliament

---

'If the Royal Family want to indulge in opinion polls, they should be allowed to, but they shouldn't be released to the public,' he said.

Mr Soames's attack is part of a growing feeling among friends of the Royals that the family is being

undermined by an attempt to modernise its activities.

According to others in the royal circle, the Queen and the Prince of Wales have become increasingly frustrated by the Government's attempt to portray them as supporters of the Labour Government.

Downing Street let it be known that it had advised Buckingham Palace on handling the media following the death of Diana, Princess of Wales.

Labour Party spin doctors were credited with the 'touchy-feely' approach that led to her two sons shaking hands with members of the public.

The Prince of Wales is also understood to resent suggestions that he is a supporter of the Government's welfare-to-work policy.

Although the Prince's Trust backed many of the principles behind the Government's New Deal for unemployed people, this was not intended to be a political gesture.

Members of the Royal Family are required to remain strictly non-partisan in their approach to politics. The Queen is said to be resisting attempts by the Government to remove much of the pomp and ceremony surrounding the annual State Opening of Parliament.

She has made clear to the Prime Minister her strong opposition to suggestions that the State Opening should happen only once a Parliament and be stripped of much of its pageantry.

She has said that she values the occasion as a time when all parts of the constitution gather together under one roof. She also fears that any changes would strip the monarchy of much of its dignity and role within the constitution.

Half favour William as next King

71 per cent back monarchy but urge change, 59 per cent think worse of the tabloid press. By Anthony King and Robert Hardman

For the first time, an opinion poll has indicated that more than half of the British people believe Prince William should succeed to the throne in place of his father.

While there remains overwhelming support for the monarchy with only 11 per cent in favour of a republic, a large majority favours a 'more democratic and approachable' institution on Continental lines.

A special Gallup survey for *The Daily Telegraph*, carried out after Saturday's funeral of Diana, Princess of Wales, also shows that most people believe that events since the Princess's death have damaged the reputation of the Queen and the Royal Family.

The same poll indicates that the standing of the tabloid press has sunk by a far greater degree.

The findings underline a general feeling, observed by the Palace and Downing Street in recent days, that while Britain remains a staunchly monarchist society, it seeks changes in the Royal Family.

As with all polls, St James's Palace refused to comment on the survey last night. However, a friend of the Prince of Wales took a realistic view: 'The poll results no doubt reflect the nation's great pride in Prince William for performing so bravely on Saturday and it is a pride which is strongly shared by his father.'

The most striking result from the survey is a decline in support for the Prince of Wales over the past three years. When Gallup asked a similar question in 1994 only 24 per cent of respondents were in favour of him stepping aside for his son. The number believing that the throne should 'skip a generation' is now 51 per cent.

Today, 41 per cent remain convinced that the Prince of Wales should succeed. Three years ago the comparable figure was 66 per cent. This result is particularly surprising since he was associated with moves to give the Royal Family a more public profile in the days before the funeral.

The principal criticism levelled against him in the media had been for taking his sons to church on the morning after the Princess's death. However, 62 per cent believe this decision was right.

Although 64 per cent of Gallup's respondents say they still respect the Royal Family, an increase on the mid-1990s, a substantial majority, 53 per cent, believe 'events of the past ten days have done damage to the public standing of the Queen and the Royal Family'.

A similar proportion, 55 per cent, say Earl Spencer did intend to criticise the Royal Family in his funeral address and, in addition, that he was right to do so.

Gallup's findings suggest something approaching a consensus on the need for modernisation of the monarchy and the Royal Family. Three years ago, 54 per cent held that view, with 29 per cent believing they 'should stay pretty much as they are now'. Today, 71 per cent favour a more democratic monarchy, with 15 per cent in favour of the *status quo*.

The Palace can derive satisfaction from the fact that events surrounding the funeral did nothing

---

The only institution to suffer more than the Royal Family as a result of the Princess's death is the tabloid press

---

for the republican cause. Only 11 per cent favour a republic – against 12 per cent supporting the idea in 1994. And no less than 83 per cent backed a law to give greater privacy to the Royal Family and other public figures.

The only institution to suffer more than the Royal Family as a result of the Princess's death is the tabloid press. No less than 59 per cent of people say their opinion of tabloids such as the *Sun*, the *Mirror* and the *Daily Mail* has 'gone down' as a result of what has happened.

Both the Palace and the Prime Minister will now be keen to enhance the standing of the Prince of Wales in the months ahead.

In the past few days, Tony Blair has established a considerable rapport with the Prince, who earlier this year had been attacked by Conservatives for being too closely associated with certain Labour projects.

Despite the Prince's successes with the Prince's Trust and his heavy programme of engagements, it is clear that the Prince's perceived differences with his former wife remain uppermost in the mind of a public deeply distressed by her death.

Certainly, the Royal Family would not countenance tampering with the line of succession in this way. And both the family and the Government would be loath to set a precedent which would play into republican hands and place an intolerable burden on Prince William.

Any such move before the death of the Queen would also have serious financial implications. The Prince of Wales receives no public funds but derives his income from the Duchy of Cornwall which can only be held by a reigning monarch's eldest son who must also be heir to the throne.   *© Telegraph Group Limited London, 1997*

Remote and stuffy royals must change

ICM poll findings by Peter Kellner

What sort of monarchy do we want? Or would we now prefer to do without one altogether? The death of Diana, Princess of Wales, has triggered the most intense debate on this subject since the abdication 61 years ago of Edward VIII.

In its poll for the *Observer*, ICM offered people four options. Two involved the retention of the monarchy, two its demise.

The verdict could scarcely be clearer: 86 per cent want to keep the monarchy, while 12 per cent would prefer Britain to become a republic. (Only 2 per cent offered ICM no opinion; when 'don't knows' are so few, it means that the issue is one that engages most of the adult population.)

But when the pro-monarchy majority is divided into its two components, the urgency of the Royal Family's need to change becomes apparent. Twelve per cent want the monarchy to 'continue in its present form', while 74 per cent think that it should 'continue but be modernised'.

What, though, does 'modernisation' mean? Does the Royal Family need to revamp its lifestyle and public image, or should it rethink its constitutional role? Or should it do both?

ICM tested a series of propositions. What emerges is a broad consensus: a majority want a less formal monarchy that is more in touch with the wider public, and only a few want the Queen to lose her constitutional role.

What irks most people is not the way she conducts her public duties as Head of State, but a deeply felt sense that she and her family are stuffy and remote.

Seventy-nine per cent agree that 'the Royal Family is out of touch with ordinary people in Britain'; three-quarters of that group 'agree a lot'.

Likewise, 62 per cent 'agree a lot' that the Royal Family should shed some of their traditional ways and become more informal; a further 19 per cent 'agree a little'. Die-hard traditionalists who 'disagree a lot' made up a mere 7 per cent.

On field sports there is also a majority (52 per cent) who 'agree a lot' that the Royal Family should give them up; at the other end of the scale only 10 per cent 'disagree a lot'.

Our poll refutes the widely held view that there is a generation gap of older people being keener than younger men and women to preserve the monarchy and its traditional ways.

ICM's figures find little or no significant differences in the attitudes among different age groups; if anything, people aged under 35 were actually less keen than the generation of their parents on converting Britain into a republic.

There is, however, one specific instance of a gender gap. Men divide evenly on whether Prince Charles or his son, Prince William, should succeed to the throne when the Queen dies. Women, however, were two-to-one in William's favour.

ICM interviewed a random sample of 511 adults by telephone throughout Britain on Wednesday and Thursday.

© *The Observer*
September, 1997

Verdict on the monarchy

1. How many marks out of 10 would you give the Queen as Britain's head of state and Prince Charles as Prince of Wales for the way they carry out their roles?

% giving 10 out of 10	1981	1997
Queen	71	10
Charles	58	5

2. Which of these options would you prefer?

	1997
a) The monarchy should continue in its present form	12
b) The monarchy should continue but be modernised	74
c) The monarchy should be replaced with a republic when the Queen dies	5
d) The monarchy should be replaced with a republic as soon as possible	7

3. Assuming that the monarchy continues, do you agree or disagree with each of these statements?

	Agree	Disagree
a) The Royal Family should become much more informal, and less concerned with preserving their traditional ways	81	15
b) The Royal Family is out of touch with ordinary people in Britain	79	17
c) The Royal Family should not take part in field sports such as fox-hunting and grouse shooting	62	23
d) The Queen should start to give interviews like other public figures	49	39
e) The Queen should give up functions such as signing new laws, opening Parliament and formally appointing a Prime Minister and stick to purely ceremonial duties	37	57

4. If the monarchy does continue, when the Queen dies, do you think that the crown should pass to Prince Charles or straight to Prince William?

Charles	38
William	53

Source: Observer / ICM

Queen to move out of the Palace

'Buck House' will be royal art gallery in significant gesture towards change. By Stephen Castle, Political Editor

The Queen will move out of Buckingham Palace to make way for a gallery devoted to the royal art collection, under plans being considered by senior court officials.

The dramatic move is a key option in a palace document on modernisation of the monarchy, due to be completed in the first part of next year. It comes in the wake of repeated calls for the Royal Family to modernise itself in the wake of the death of Diana, Princess of Wales.

Leaving the palace would not be a great personal blow to the Queen, who has always been said to dislike the large and soulless building, preferring to spend weekends at Windsor. Prince Charles, too, is thought to dislike the palace. The Queen's London base could move to St James's or Kensington Palace or to Clarence House, the Queen Mother's residence.

They have a suite of 12 rooms at Buckingham Palace, out of about 600 rooms in total, housing an administrative staff of about 850 and various members of the royal household.

A move from Buckingham Palace is likely to win immediate backing from the Government. Chris Smith, Secretary of State for Culture, Media and Sport, has already asked the palace whether it can make more of the priceless royal art collection, which includes works by Rubens, Canaletto, Vermeer and Leonardo da Vinci, available to the public.

The monarchy reform process, being conducted by the Way Ahead group, consisting of family members and palace officials, has been accelerated in the wake of Diana's death. Last week's demonstration of openness by the Queen and the Duke of Edinburgh during their Golden Wedding celebrations is being portrayed as evidence of the Royal Family's wish to reform itself.

The new, more personal style has been encouraged by Downing Street, and the relationship between the Queen's private secretary, Sir Robert Fellowes, and the Prime Minister's press secretary, Alastair Campbell, is said to be good.

> *Buckingham Palace has 45 acres of garden – large enough for parties which have entertained 9,000 guests at a time*

The Culture Secretary has been suggesting a series of possibilities for the royal art collection, including the loan of art works to regional galleries. But royal advisers see moving from the palace as an opportunity to make a significant gesture to underline the Royal Family's commitment to a smaller-scale, more modern operation. The move would help answer criticisms about the costs of the royals, and Prince Charles, regarded as a 'moderniser', is likely to back the change.

If the palace is converted into a 'living gallery' or 'people's palace', it would be closed to the public for state occasions. Otherwise it would allow viewing of a fine art collection – much of it now hidden from public view – which includes masterpieces by Van Dyck, De Hooch, Michelangelo and Rembrandt, as well as sculpture by Canova.

Buckingham Palace has 45 acres of garden – large enough for parties which have entertained 9,000 guests at a time. Additions include lifts, swimming pool, a cinema and nuclear shelter.

John Major has agreed to act for Princes William and Harry to help resolve a legal wrangle over Diana's will. The former Prime Minister's role as a special 'guardian' is thought desirable because the Princess had not changed her will after her divorce from the Prince of Wales.

© Independent on Sunday November, 1997

Embattled Royal Family may reduce its ranks

The Palace's think-tank is facing some hard options in its efforts to improve its tarnished image, reports Robert Hardman

Since its inception four years ago, the Way Ahead group has addressed a broad range of royal subjects ranging from Roman Catholics in the family to the finer points of flag-flying.

On most issues, there is usually a swift consensus and a ready acceptance of the need for certain changes.

One question, however, has proved very difficult for the twice-yearly assemblies of senior members of the Royal Family and senior courtiers, but is one which the group is now determined to answer: how do we shrink 'The Firm'?

The Victorian model of an extended family of royal personages was fine for an age when there was an Empire to tour and dynastic marriages to be made. But, as society has seen the extended family give way to the modern 'nuclear' family unit, the House of Windsor has found itself under increasing pressure to follow suit.

For the Queen, this is a painful process. She is well aware of the unsung work carried out by her cousins who were unable to follow conventional careers in their youth by the royal conventions of the day.

Last year, for example, the Duke and Duchess of Gloucester carried out 400 engagements between them and there are thousands of small charities and institutions for whom there is nothing 'minor' about the 'minor royal' who happens to be their patron.

In 1975, however, the Queen agreed to take on the public costs of her cousins' annuities, previously met by the Treasury.

Since 1993, she has done the same for all members of the Royal Family except Queen Elizabeth, the Queen Mother and Prince Philip, who continue to be supported by the state. The Prince of Wales is self-sufficient thanks to the Duchy of Cornwall.

But detailed market research commissioned by the Palace has shown that the public still regards the family as 'wasteful' and 'out of touch'.

Officials are also well aware that the 10-year Civil List arrangements laid down in 1990 will soon be up for renewal and that a major public debate on royal finances is inevitable.

> *Much of the problem in countering hostile public perceptions, however, is a simple one of communication*

If the Palace acts now, it may deflect much of the criticism when the Civil List debate occurs in 2000. At present, the focus is on how large the active Royal Family should be rather than the finer financial points.

It is generally agreed that, in future, this will consist of the sovereign, his or her children and the children of the heir to the throne.

The Queen and Prince Philip are known to be of the opinion that it would be wrong to strip their cousins, now approaching pension-

able age, of a royal style and status which has been theirs all their lives.

The stumbling block is the Duke of York's daughters who are presently Their Royal Highnesses. Many courtiers take the view that it is inconsistent for the children of the Princess Royal to be commoners while their cousins are royal, particularly since Princess Beatrice, nine, and Princess Eugenie, seven, will have no official royal role as adults.

It is also argued that, since the ancient rules of male primogeniture are now to be overturned in favour of a 'unisex' arrangement, it is perverse to confer royal status on the children of a monarch's son but not a monarch's daughter.

If the two Princesses are to lose their royal status, it must be done so as not to appear vindictive. But the Duchess of York would appear to see the logic of it, judging by yesterday's reports that she would accept such a change provided that it became a general rule. This would then also apply to any children that Prince Edward might have.

To royal critics such as Alan Williams, the Labour MP for Swansea West, such reforms are mere 'tinkering with the edges'.

The Way Ahead group is certainly aware of the need for more substantial reforms to the royal bill.

These are likely to involve an exodus of the royal cousins from Kensington Palace with new homes and some sort of pension provided at the Queen's personal expense. The security and transport costs of the so-called minor royals will also be subject to more stringent review.

Much of the problem in countering hostile public perceptions, however, is a simple one of communication. The fact that the royal household has shaved millions off the Palace bill since it took over maintenance duties from the Government, or that royal travel has been streamlined, or that the Queen is a cheaper head of state than the German president, is barely known.

Hence, the impending appointment of a 'director of communications' at Buckingham Palace. While the occupant is not expected to be a 'spin doctor', he or she is likely to try to play up the Palace's pro-active nature and to dispel the widespread view that the Royal Family only changes when it receives a hefty kick from public opinion. This time, the Palace wants to undertake reform and to be seen generating it.

For example, some ministers are presently taking the credit for a plan to alter the rules of primogeniture so that a sovereign's eldest child succeeds to the throne regardless of sex.

Since the death of Diana, Princess of Wales, there has been nothing to suggest that the public is less royalist but it is certainly now more expectant of change

---

It will doubtless go down as one of the historic reforming measures of the Blair administration, yet it simply absorbs private legislation proposed by Lord Archer last year. And where did the idea first surface? At a Way Ahead meeting in 1995.

Courtiers still recall with anger the handling of the 1992 announcement that the Queen was to pay tax.

This was something which officials had been planning for years but it appeared at the time that the Queen was reluctantly caving in to media and political demands.

A good indication of the lack of communication is illustrated by the Queen's writing to her Lord Lieutenants to remind them that bowing and curtseying is optional.

This has always been the case, but to read some reports over the weekend, it is as if some draconian medieval law is about to be repealed.

Since the death of Diana, Princess of Wales, there has been nothing to suggest that the public is less royalist but it is certainly now more expectant of change.

The Royal Family is clearly keen to stay one step ahead of public opinion in enacting that change.

The saving of the monarchy

By Hugo Young

The Princess is dead and buried: long live her successors. Going to her grave, that's where she has left the monarchy. Last week was unique for many things, and unforgettable in the experience of many people. Among its defining properties, however, none will last longer than the life it breathed into royalism. Republicans, eat your hearts out. What happened, in the end, was a triumph for royalty, not the disaster many diagnosed at first; proof of royalist ardour, not the beginning of the end of the magic.

The week was spent in fantasyland, a theatre of pleasure as well as pain. Royalty takes the place of religion in sating, in the British case, all people's need of myths. But let's not continue the fantasy into the realm of post-funereal judgement. If I were a serious republican, I'd have to concede that all the excitable talk about monarchy being on the verge of destruction by the popular will was rendered ridiculous by the spectacle of 2 million people crying

their eyes out on Saturday. Has there been a more breathless case of wishful thinking than the notion of this life and death being a platform for the ultimate constitutional reform?

There were bits of Saturday's beautiful ceremonial that showed royalism, and all who march with her, on the back foot. When the Queen and her little clan went down to the palace gates to watch the coffin pass, they seemed a depleted bunch. Dragged down to the people's level, they didn't know how to look. Compelled to be ordinary, they lost so much of what their separateness bestows.

Republicans, eat your hearts out. What happened, in the end, was a triumph for royalty, not the disaster many diagnosed at first

---

Earl Spencer, also, socked them. Never has a figure of total obscurity more brilliantly seized his moment to deliver a message to the world. It won't quickly be forgotten, even though he chooses exile from the country in which he couldn't cut it. What the earl had to say about the hunter-killers in the media spoke for what many people think they think. What he implied about the record of the royal family as rearers of happy children, and their need for help from another dynastic line, was laid out vividly before us in the marital wreckage scattered round the front pews. But monarchy? The tumbrels rolling, by popular demand? Royalty, royalism, royal-ness, all the forms and declensions of the regal, in jeopardy? And proven to be so by the quality of Britain's emotional apocalypse?

Not only is that an improbable political conclusion to draw about the most conservative country on Earth, it seems to me utterly to misread what's going on out there in the hearts of men and women. It's the fanciful conceit of those who think there can be no proper reform of ancient Britain without the ending of the monarchy, joined by those who have such contempt for what happened to Diana at the hands of the royal family that they believe the only redemption is to be found in abolition.

The Princess wasn't a movie star. She wasn't Madonna. If she had been, her death would have been a one-day wonder. If she hadn't been a royal, she would have been close to nothing in the calendar of celebrity. Only accoutred with royal status did she gain access first to the people's fascination, then to their adoration, finally to their imagined love. She was beautiful, a consummate populist. She acquired a large part of her identity, and much of her popularity, by being perceived to fight the royal family, after being atrociously victimised by them. She was the best of the royals but what mattered, miles ahead of everything, was the royal. Only royalty reaches the millions and ties bouquets to railings up and down the land.

So what happened last week turns out not to be the end of monarchy but, more likely, its rebirth. That depends on the learning of lessons, which the incumbents will find very difficult to absorb. You can't invent public warmth in a 71-year-old woman who has made an ideology out of enshrining what is past. You can't discover overnight a capacity for popular connection in a stiff, neurotic, autocratic middle-aged man who, in the verdict his late wife gave to the editor of the *New Yorker*, was not born to lead the country but to hold house-parties for artists in Tuscany. None the less, such loosening-up, such levelling-down, the improvement not the death of royalty is what will surely now be attempted.

For this task, the royals have the right prime minister on hand. Tony Blair, it should always be recalled, is a social and political conservative. No particle of him has even the smallest leaning towards anything so radical as the end of the monarchy. His constitutional reform programme, though in the British

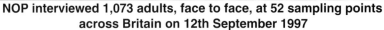

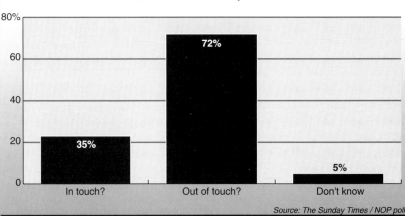

Some say the Queen is in touch with the feelings of the British people, others say she is remote and out of touch, is she?

NOP interviewed 1,073 adults, face to face, at 52 sampling points across Britain on 12th September 1997

Source: The Sunday Times / NOP poll

context portrayable as almost revolutionary, is in fact pretty modest. Only when the Blair Government provides for an elected second chamber, and a fully proportional electoral system, will we know they have judged the rules of our politics, the constitution, to be radically defective: a judgement which the years of incumbency will soon, I confidently predict, debar them from endorsing.

Blair is an ameliorist. He wants to make things better but without changing anything in a way that alarms too many people or, indeed, makes a single identifiable enemy. You can find many positive things to say about him, but his desire to challenge fundamental preconceptions is pretty limited. This is as true of his approach to the pillars of the constitution as it is of anything. What interests him is advancing what is practical, feasible, not unpopular. It does not necessarily have to be congruent with some grand doctrinal scheme. Clauses and canons are anathema to his way of politics. He's not interested in the

---

So what happened last week turns out not to be the end of monarchy but, more likely, its rebirth

---

text-books and the theories and the wonderful constructs that hope to render the monarchy terminally illogical. He is monarchy's most potent friend.

But that's also because he, too, is a populist. His entire political record has been based on an understanding of what the people want and, even allowing for the preposterous excesses the voting system can produce, his majority in April proved a point. What the people showed every sign of wanting last week wasn't no monarchy, not the ersatz aridities of republicanism, not some man-made artefact that would preserve them from all that emotion: but a better monarchy, a monarchy that came down to their level without depriving them of residual awe, a monarch whose passing might reliably command a display of national grief half-matching that accorded to Diana.

Adaptation, the Blairite watch-word for almost everything, is the name of the royalist game as well. It's the quality that has kept this country, for better or for worse, conservative. In the 18th and the 19th centuries, our kings did not have their heads chopped off, when all around were losing theirs. If this fate is spared them in the 21st century, Diana will have played her part, in death as in life, by jolting them, at the final hour, into doing what the people want them to do. Ask not for whom the bell tolls, it tolls for the republic.

© *The Guardian*
September, 1997

Royal Family is regaining public esteem

By Anthony King

Events since the death of Diana, Princess of Wales – notably the Queen and Prince Philip's golden wedding celebrations – have slowed and may even have arrested the recent decline in public esteem for the Royal Family, according to Gallup's latest survey for *The Daily Telegraph*.

They also appear to have enhanced the personal standing of the Prince of Wales. The proportion of people believing the Queen should at some stage abdicate in the Prince's favour has risen sharply over the past year while the proportion believing the Prince of Wales should stand aside in favour of his elder son has fallen.

Gallup has asked at intervals since the Queen's *annus horribilis*, 1992: Has your personal opinion of the Royal Family gone up or gone down over the past year? Almost no one between 1992 and 1996 said they held the Royal Family in higher esteem than the year before but that proportion has risen to 25 per cent.

The proportion saying their opinion of the Royal Family has gone down remains high – 41 per cent in the latest survey – but that figure has fallen sharply as the other has increased. A year ago, 52 per cent of Gallup's respondents said their opinion had gone down.

> **Almost no one between 1992 and 1996 said they held the Royal Family in higher esteem than the year before but that proportion has risen to 25 per cent**

The Prince of Wales seems to have won large numbers of friends for himself and his family during his recent South African visit. Asked whether 'the Queen should or should not abdicate in favour of the Prince sometime within the next few years', only 19 per cent a year ago said she should. That figure has now risen to 30 per cent.

However, a clear majority, 65 per cent, would still prefer the Queen to remain on the throne for the foreseeable future.

On the much canvassed option of 'skipping a generation', opinion has also shifted. In the immediate aftermath of the Princess's funeral last September, the number of those believing the Prince of Wales should stand aside in favour of Prince William rose to 51 per cent. However, it has now fallen back to 41 per cent.

A clear majority, though not an overwhelming one, 54 per cent, now believes the Prince of Wales should succeed to the throne in the usual way. As recently as last September, the figure was only 41 per cent.

In its recent survey, the Gallup Poll conducted telephone interviews with 1,011 adults across Great Britain.

• Anthony King is Professor of Government at Essex University.

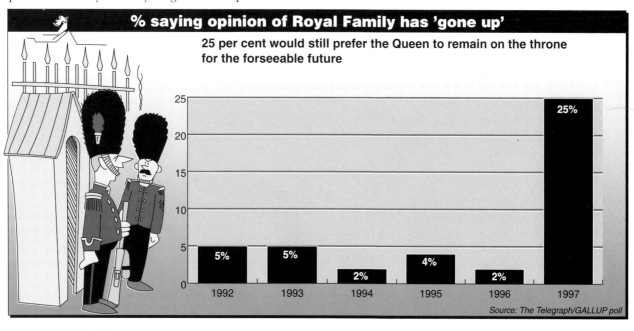

% saying opinion of Royal Family has 'gone up'

25 per cent would still prefer the Queen to remain on the throne for the forseeable future

1992	1993	1994	1995	1996	1997
5%	5%	2%	4%	2%	25%

Source: The Telegraph/GALLUP poll

A word from two groups

We invited two organisations on opposite sides of the monarchy versus republic debate in Australia to summarise their key concerns. These are not the only important voices in the debate, but their views illustrate opposing opinions.

Australians for Constitutional Monarchy provided this article on why Australia should not become a republic

'Australia is the world's sixth oldest continuous democracy after Britain, USA, Canada, Switzerland and Sweden. Four of the six are constitutional monarchies and four have British origins. In 2001 Australia will celebrate 100 years of our working Constitution which made us a nation in 1901.

Prior to 1901 our land was divided into separate colonies. Throughout the 19th century our ancestors debated the best system of government which would create a unified and stable nation. The very best ideas were taken from constitutions all over the world and the result was Federation, and the Australian Constitution, proudly our own. Our Constitution has been the heartbeat of our nation ever since. It is the heart of our Australian identity.

We have no reason to change the system which has served us so well.

We are a peaceful, friendly, democratic and stable society which has seen people from all over the world choose Australia as their home. We should not risk changing something that works so well.

To become a republic would require making at least 70 changes to our Constitution, according to the Republic Advisory Committee Report. It will mean a new theory and system of government. Why do it?

Our present system works well. It keeps the politicians in order. It is far safer to stay with a proven system than to experiment with an untried alternative

---

We already have an Australian Head of State who is above party politics, the Governor-General, who is nominated by the Prime Minister of the day, and in each State we have a Premier-nominated Governor.

As our Australian head of State and Constitutional umpire, the Governor-General can and has dismissed the Prime Minister. The Queen of Australia cannot. Both are above party politics.

The president of a republic, however elected, will be a politician and will wear the colours of one of the teams. This could lead to unstable governments as power struggles develop between a political president and a political prime minister.

Australia is one federal nation with six States. Under the republicans there will be a president in every State, a total of seven republics. And which of the 116 republics across the world do they want for us? Republicans still cannot agree on the important details.

A republic will not improve unemployment, the environment, or our national debt. But it will change our flag, our national anthem, the RAN, RAR and RAAF. Many republicans say it will change us – but to what?

SYDNEY Newsagent

DAME EDNA EVERAGE TO BECOME QUEEN OF AUSTRALIA

Ken Pyne

Australia is closely linked to the international community. Our history has made us what we are – a free, tolerant and diverse people with a working democracy. The Queen as Head of the Commonwealth, unites 1.6 billion people in 53 countries. As separately, Queen of Canada, Queen of New Zealand, Queen of Papua New Guinea or Queen of Australia, in each country's affairs she relies only on advice from that country's Prime Minister. Each country operates totally independently under its own Governor-General.

A republic will put at risk what we now enjoy: our political stability, our national unity, our flag and our national anthem. In other words, Australia as we know it.

A republic will also cost financially and emotionally. The Republic Advisory Committee estimated in 1994 that a popularly elected president would cost $45 million minimum each election. It didn't publish the additional costs for elections in the six States, of the presidential entourage, travel expenses, planning the presidential palace, etcetera.

Our present system works well. It keeps the politicians in order. It is far safer to stay with a proven system than to experiment with an untried alternative.

Australia is already a proud, independent, sovereign nation. The republicans base their arguments on the need to have an Australian as Head of State. We already have an Australian as Head of State – so why risk change.'

The Australian Republic Movement provided this article on why Australia should become a republic
'Our Head of State should represent Australia, our national unity and our unique Australian values of freedom, tolerance and a fair go.

Thanks to the courage and hard work of Australians, we live in the best country in the world. So why should Australia's Head of State be the King or Queen of England? Why is no Australian good enough to be our Head of State?

Shouldn't every Australian child be able to aspire to hold any Australian public office? Does it still make sense for our parliamentarians and judges to swear allegiance, not to Australia, but to the Queen?

The Australian Republican Movement believes we should encourage all Australians, especially our children, to be prouder of and more committed to their country and its values. In a diverse nation like ours it is important everyone can identify with our national institutions and that they represent Australia, not another country.

Every hundred years we get a chance to make a change. As proud Australians, we should enter the new century with one of our own citizens as Head of State

---

Queen Elizabeth is admired and respected by Australians. However, she is not an Australian and does not live here. She is seen, around the world, as the Queen of England. When she visits other countries she does so as the British Head of State and promotes, very effectively, the sale of British goods.

Our Governor-General does a good job, but he will always be seen as only the Queen's deputy.

This change would involve replacing the Queen (and the Governor-General) with an Australian citizen as Head of State chosen by, and in touch with, Australians.

Our present system of justice, based on British common law, and of federal parliamentary government with a Prime Minister answerable to Parliament would remain exactly the way it is today.

Our flag, our national anthem and the name of our country would not be changed. We would remain a member of the British Commonwealth and compete in the Commonwealth Games. Our friendly relations with Great Britain would continue.

In fact most Commonwealth countries already have their own Head of State.

An Australian Head of State need involve no additional expense. The present budget and accommodation for the office of Governor-General are more than sufficient.

As is now the case with the Queen (and her representative the Governor-General) the main functions of the Head of State would be ceremonial. The Head of State would normally act only on the advice of the Prime Minister and would have the same powers as the Governor-General which would be carefully spelled out in the Constitution.

As to the method of appointing the new Head of State, the ARM does not have a closed mind and looks forward to the Convention considering different modes of appointment, including direct election by the people. The ARM recommends appointing the new Head of State by a two-thirds majority of a joint sitting of the Federal Parliament supported by both the Government and Opposition. That would ensure the appointee could always command broad community support and would not be an ex-politician. At the moment the Governor-General is appointed by the Prime Minister alone.

The ARM believes that a majority of Australians already want to have an Australian as their Head of State. If the Constitutional Convention confirms this, the ARM believes the Federal Parliament should waste no time in preparing the appropriate amendments to the Constitution and putting them to the people for their approval in a constitutional referendum. This could happen in the course of 1998.

Every hundred years we get a chance to make a change. As proud Australians, we should enter the new century with one of our own citizens as Head of State. Let's get on with it!'

© Australians for Constitutional Monarchy and The Australian Republic Movement, 1997

Mounted opposition

Is Canada the next crown defector?

We need a more effective head of state. Fulfilling more than just a ceremonial role, heads of state play a vital part in a country's day-to-day life. Certainly, the Queen has performed this function well in Britain. However, she has not had the same effect here. She cannot adequately fill the same role for a faraway country in which she doesn't even reside.

The Governor-General, as the Queen's representative in Canada, is supposed to pick up the slack. It could have become an effective office had we continued appointing distinguished Canadians. However well we started, it has become patronage for friends of the incumbent Prime Minister. It's time to change that.

Setting up our own monarchy here in Canada isn't realistic. The solution is to become a republic. Many believe that would mean an American-style system, when most want to continue with a parliamentary system. We can become a republic without sacrificing parliamentary democracy.

How do we set up the republic? The first step is to bug the politicians – they won't move on the issue unless they feel motivated by public opinion to do so. The second step is to have the necessary amendments made. It would require the approval of all ten provincial governments. A plebiscite would be held. The premier of each province would have to respect the wishes of the voters and, if approved in his province, would be obligated to ask the legislature to approve the change. I am quite confident that a plebiscite would find a majority in favour of a republic in each province.

It may be too late for us to catch up with the Australians, but there is no reason why we cannot have a Canadian republic. It can be done, if it has the support of Canadians from all walks of life.

Kevin McDougald

In the Minister's words

I recently received a letter from Industry Minister John Manley, in which the minister makes clear his position on the future of the monarchy in Canada.

Dear Mr McDougald,
Thank you for your letter in support of my comments on the Monarchy. I regret the delay in replying.

Early in September, I gave an interview with the *Vancouver Sun* regarding Canada's future in the information economy. At the close of the half-hour session, I was asked to confirm that what the reporter had heard were my views concerning the Senate and the Monarchy. I responded honestly.

Since then, there has been extensive media coverage of my comments. You should know that contrary to speculation, this was not a contrived attempt by the government to float any 'trial balloons'.

In the original interview, I expressed my personal view that when Queen Elizabeth's reign ends,

> *Of the 53 member nations of the Commonwealth, only 16 retain the Queen as Head of State, although she is Head of the Commonwealth*

we should consider selecting a truly Canadian head of state who will promote and represent Canada's interests both at home and abroad.

My opinions are not a rejection of the Monarchy, but an acknowledgement that the world and Canada's place in it is not static. Australia has a constitutional convention discussing a republic. The British are undergoing significant constitutional change; referenda recently took place in Scotland and Wales. Even Prime Minister Tony Blair has referred to changes in the role and function of the Monarchy.

As global political structures are constantly evolving, it is not inappropriate to consider the advantages of having a Canadian head of state. If we do so, I am certain it would not be limited to Protestants, nor would males be preferred over females, as is the case with the British succession.

It is interesting to note that of the 53 member nations of the Commonwealth, only 16 retain the Queen as Head of State, although she is Head of the Commonwealth.

Canadians are considering various issues and debates that will have a significant impact on our national identity. While it is not a pressing concern, the role of the Monarchy is worthy of a broader public discussion. I do not expect all Canadians to share my view; my goal is simply to encourage useful discussion.

I hope that I have clarified my position. Thank you for taking the time to share your opinion on this matter.

Yours very truly,
John Manley

You must earn your keep, Royals told

Civil List shake-up will mean only working family members get cash. By Joe Murphy, Political Editor

The Civil List is to be replaced by a new arrangement which rewards only those Royals who regularly perform public duties.

In a fundamental break with tradition, they will no longer be entitled to taxpayers' support merely by being born into the Royal Family.

Instead, plans are being drawn up at Buckingham Palace to radically reform the 240-year-old system by which the State pays the Monarchy and which insiders concede is farcical.

At present, 11 Royals are paid from the list, but for the past five years the Queen has refunded the taxpayer for all but herself, Prince Philip and the Queen Mother.

This arrangement began in 1993 when there was an outcry over taxpayers' outlay of £1.5 million a year for minor Royals. But it was considered to be only a temporary measure until a review of the entire system could be carried out.

The intention now is that payments to minor Royals should reflect their commitment to public service. Such a reform of the list, which dates back to 1760, would also underline that the trappings of Royalty go hand in hand with full-time public service – making clear that high birth alone is not enough.

'There could be a clear demarcation line which members of the Royal Family could opt in or out of,' said a senior source.

'Those who perform a full list of engagements would naturally be supported and transported. Others might choose to support themselves.'

Initially, the taxpayer would not gain because of the Queen's decision to refund the payments to most of her family. But it would make it easier to slim down the list in future.

And it is thought it would reassure the public that the Royals were meeting their obligations to public service – in effect, giving value for money.

> **'Those who perform a full list of engagements would naturally be supported and transported. Others might choose to support themselves'**

It could also pave the way for a reduction in the perks enjoyed by minor Royals, including free flights within the UK. Cutting out such expenditure is considered a priority by Palace reformers, who feel the Monarchy must keep pace with public opinion.

The plans are entirely the work of Palace modernisers and Downing Street has not yet been officially consulted. However, Tony Blair is understood to approve of the debate.

Negotiations are under way because a 10-year agreement on payments reached under John Major expires in 2001.

The Civil List has been racked by controversy. It was originally provided by Parliament in return for Crown Estate revenues (currently about £100 million a year) going to the Treasury. Prior to that the King also paid the wage bill for judges, ambassadors and Royal officers.

Later the Treasury paid the wages of public officials, plus a reduced Civil List.

Fresh controversy arose during the high-inflation years of the Seventies when annual upratings of the payments became necessary.

© *Mail on Sunday*
March, 1998

The Civil List

About 70 per cent of Civil List expenditure goes to pay the salaries of staff working directly for The Queen.

The Queen	The Queen Mother	The Duke of Edinburgh	Total
£7,900,000	£643,000	£359,000	£8,902,000

Paid from the Civil List

The Queen refunds money to Treasury:

The Duke of York	£249,000
Prince Edward	£96,000
The Princess Royal	£228,000
Princess Margaret	£219,000
Princess Alice	£87,000
Duke of Gloucester	£175,000
Duke of Kent	£236,000
Princess Alexandra	£225,000

Source: The Mail on Sunday

Why the Queen should abdicate . . .

it's as natural as retirement. By Anne McElvoy

The V & A once advertised itself as an excellent café with some nice art attached. Now that Kensington Palace is rumoured to be turning into a picture gallery, we are on our way to getting another nice museum with a monarchy attached. So many reformist ideas are leaking from government and the Palace's consultative Way Ahead group that, far from following Bagehot's instruction to never let daylight in on the magic, royalty is dwelling in the unrelenting glare of critical scrutiny.

How strong public dissatisfaction remains was shown in a leaked poll which led the Palace to conclude that a spin-doctor – contemporary form of the genie – should be appointed. The *Sun* revealed that the opening of Parliament is to be simplified, HRH's culled and curtseying abandoned. Not even in the advanced condition of Tony Blair's love-in with Rupert Murdoch has the *Sun* become the official journal of record (yet), but the stories were well sourced and the denials vague.

The death of the Princess of Wales was an event after which, in Yeats's words, 'all is changed, utterly'. It was inconceivable that the Royal Family could simply go on as if nothing had happened. From the moment that Mr Blair made his intuitive leap and spoke of Diana as the 'People's Princess', it was clear that his government would take a defining role in the future of the Crown. But my strong suspicion is that the impetus to form a reformist alliance came as much from the Prince of Wales. Indeed, he may have thought of it first.

Even before Diana's death, Prince Charles was aware that the monarchy needed to be reinvigorated to ensure its survival. In New Labour, he saw a potent ally for change. If there is one thing that we can all

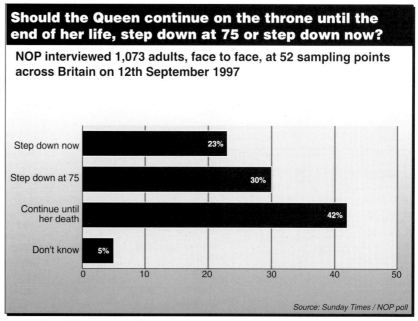

Should the Queen continue on the throne until the end of her life, step down at 75 or step down now?

NOP interviewed 1,073 adults, face to face, at 52 sampling points across Britain on 12th September 1997

- Step down now: 23%
- Step down at 75: 30%
- Continue until her death: 42%
- Don't know: 5%

Source: Sunday Times / NOP poll

agree Mr Blair is good at, it is managing change. When the Prince first met Peter Mandelson, he remarked, 'Ah, the red nose man', a reference to Mr Mandelson's deft decision to replace the implied militancy of the red flag with the inclusive symbolism of a well-loved flower.

After the election Mr Mandelson, who can be charming when he wants to be, was sent to dine with Camilla Parker Bowles, while the MP Tony Wright, acting as the Lord Chancellor's emissary, was given leave to condemn those Anglican clergymen who seek to block a remarriage by the heir to the throne.

It struck me at the time that the logic of this partnership ran in one direction only; it strengthened Prince Charles's chance of becoming king before the death of his mother. Although custom and loyalty forbid that he say it, this is what he wants. It would be highly unnatural for any man in middle age, whose life has been one long preparation for a job, not to wish that the time would come to get to work. How much keenly the Prince must feel this now, as the winds of change whistle under the

stout oak doors of Windsor. The response to Diana's death confirmed that we are a far less deferential, less conformist nation than we were. For the first time this century, a mass of people expressed public dissatisfaction with a remote, inward-looking royal family.

One powerful paradox of Thatcherism was that it undermined conservative attitudes in society. Nothing was left unquestioned. It tore up old ways of thinking and working and behaving. Cherie Blair's failure to curtsey to the Queen was an instructive, a representative lapse. We do not see why we should leave traditions intact where they no longer serve us well. We look at our monarchy and ask whether it provides what we, the people, want of it. At last, we are behaving like citizens, not subjects.

Initiatives to scale down the size of the Royal Family follow, some fifty years on, my grandfather's unwanted advice that it should rid itself of the 'hangers on' (he agreed to help support King George, his wife and children, 'but that's the lot'). It should certainly rid itself fast of the royal version of Clause IV – to bar to an eldest daughter inheriting the throne.

There is still, however, one great unspoken: the future of the Queen herself. It is absurd nowadays for a monarch to rule until death, a remnant of the belief in the divine right of kings. Otherwise, only the president of the National Union of Mineworkers keeps his jobs for life, and much good that has done his members. In short, it is time for the Queen to consider retirement. To use the word abdication – heavy with woeful echoes of Edward VIII – is to invite misunderstanding. Queen Elizabeth is over 70 years old. She has ruled for 46 years. The millennium is approaching. What better time for a generational shift?

I imagine that this proposal is unwelcome to her. She took the throne for life. Few older people revise such fundamental attitudes. For the same reason, it is cruel to expect that she will rise to the challenge of forging a thoroughly modern monarchy. She was subjected to a 'People's' wedding anniversary party and endured it with forbearance. But the community-centre style and Mr Blair's Gawd-bless-you- Ma'am tribute did not suit her. A still, small voice inside must

have thought, 'What on earth am I doing here?'

Yet a less formal monarchy is what we must have. At times of constitutional upheaval, through devolution to the House of Lords, a single, non-political head of state should embody both the unity of the United Kingdom and the growing diversity of its governance. The job description has altered. That is the real reason for changing the chief executive of what Prince Philip still calls 'the Firm'.

Prince Charles understands this. He has dropped his unappealing habit of whining about his misfortunes and wishing he had been born Bob Geldof. The Prince's Trust enshrined welfare-to-work long before Gordon Brown came along. I wouldn't appoint him as London's architect-in-chief, but at least he has opinions and voices them. The objection that Mrs Parker Bowles cannot be his consort is ill-founded. She will never become queen, nor fill Diana's elegant shoes, but she is a mature and sensible woman and would not seek to do so. They should marry if they wish – a happy king is preferable to a miserable one. The wedding could be the first down-sized, low-cost royal event. If marriage brings forth calls for disestablishment, so

much the better. The church does not own the monarchy, but neither does the monarchy any longer own the church.

My Ladybird book of *Kings and Queens*, published in the mid-1970s, contained a fulsome description of the 'second Elizabethan age'. It showed the Queen boarding new-fangled aeroplanes and as head of the perfect nuclear family. How dated that seems now – as distant in some ways as the first Elizabethan era. The golden family turned out to be a nest of unhappiness. 'She's had her troubles just like I've had mine,' said an old lady in the East End last month when the Queen visited. Too right. If they weren't royal, someone would have alerted social services long ago.

But, then again, we no longer really believe in the post-1910 fiction of the monarchy as First Family. Neither – outside the rarefied echelons of Tory Anglicanism – do we see it as the untouchable source of Bagehot's magic. A monarchy that is compact, dignified and which expresses the link between all parts and peoples of the United Kingdom is the best defence against republicanism. It must change, because not to do so will mean the end of our faith in it. That is death to any institution.

© *Independent on Sunday*
March, 1998

Why the monarchy will survive

Information from the Manorial Society of Great Britain

In recent years, the prophets of gloom and doom have taken a perverse delight in predicting the end of the British monarchy and the establishment of a republic after the death of Her Majesty Queen Elizabeth II. When pressed to give reasons for such a prediction, the woolliness of their thought processes soon becomes apparent. They cite the loss of popularity and confidence in the monarchy resulting from the matrimonial tribulations of the Queen's three married children and follow this up with references to the

'cost to the taxpayer' that maintaining the monarchy allegedly involves. This last is an enduring myth which lives on no matter how many times it is pointed out that the monarchy costs the taxpayer nothing, being maintained by the revenues from the Crown Lands, which, since the reign of King George III, every sovereign has voluntarily surrendered to the government in exchange for a Civil List and whereby the government has gained the better bargain since the revenues far exceed the expenses of the monarchy and its trappings.

Characteristically, those who predict the end of the monarchy venture no suggestions of how this is to be effected. Will it be abolished by act of parliament, which the monarch of the day would be called upon to ratify, or will it follow a referendum? Imagination boggles at the thought of the cumbersome machinery and legislation which would be required to dismantle the present monarchical system and set up a republic with an elected head of state in its place. Fortunately, this country tried republicanism and got

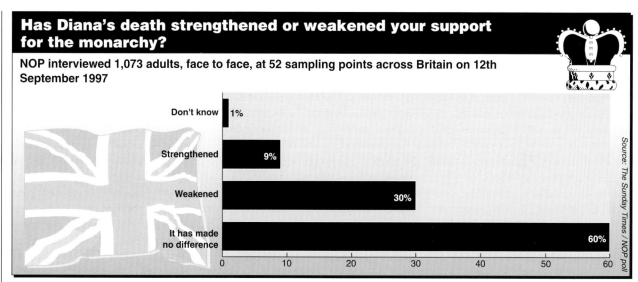

Has Diana's death strengthened or weakened your support for the monarchy?

NOP interviewed 1,073 adults, face to face, at 52 sampling points across Britain on 12th September 1997

Don't know	1%
Strengthened	9%
Weakened	30%
It has made no difference	60%

Source: The Sunday Times / NOP poll

it out of its system more than 300 years ago, long before the rise of republics elsewhere.

For the first 500 years after the Norman Conquest, monarchs were accepted without question as the natural rulers ordained by God. There were good kings and bad kings, but on the few occasions when one was deposed he was always replaced by another, any other form of government being not only unthinkable but unknown. It cannot really be said that any medieval kings were popular since little more than their names was known to the majority of the people. With the advent of the Tudors, things began to change and the introduction of realistic portraiture on the coinage ensured that the monarch's true likeness became known at last to the people. The first sovereign who can be said to have been popular was Queen Elizabeth I. Her royal progresses about the country made her known to far more of her subjects than any of her predecessors had been, and towards the end of her reign she was able to claim that she counted as its greatest glory the fact that she had reigned with her people's love.

Elizabeth's successor, the alien James I, although unprepossessing in appearance and often uncouth in manner, nevertheless managed to attain a measure of popularity, occasioned partly by his general air of affability and bonhomie and partly by recognition of his skilled statecraft. It was not for nothing that he was called 'the wisest fool in Christendom'. Under James, too, England experienced the presence of a young royal family. It was a tragedy that the godlike Henry Frederick, Prince of Wales, was cut off in his prime abroad, leaving only the sickly 'Baby Charles' to take on the burden of royalty after the death of their father. He did so convinced of his 'divine right' to rule and, despite his many mistakes which were to lead to the Civil War and the temporary abolition of the monarchy, managed to inspire an all-consuming devotion in his followers. His trial and execution dismayed far more than those who condoned them and it is recorded that when his head was severed from his body a great groan went up from the crowd surrounding the scaffold outside the Banqueting House in Whitehall, and many surged forward to dip handkerchiefs in the royal blood, thus initiating the cult of the 'Martyr King' which has persisted in one form or another to the present day. Nearly 150 years were to elapse before another European sovereign (Louis XVI of France) was destined to meet a like fate at the hands of his subjects.

The eleven years that followed Charles I's death saw Britain's first and only experiment with a

---

Characteristically, those who predict the end of the monarchy venture no suggestions of how this is to be effected

---

republican form of government, destined to become a virtual dictatorship under Oliver Cromwell, who assumed many of the trappings of the old monarchy, even to the extent of being seated in the Coronation Chair (moved from Westminster Abbey to Westminster Hall for the purpose) for his installation as Lord Protector. On Cromwell's death, his son and successor, Richard Cromwell, proved to be less than half the man his father had been, so paving the way for the restoration of King Charles II in 1660. The new monarch was received with great enthusiasm on all sides. Young, good-looking, and possessed with the Stuart charm in full measure, he won all hearts and soon proved himself to be an astute ruler well able to maintain his position. Unfortunately, his brother and successor, James II, lacked Charles's charm and was tainted by his bigoted obsession to restore the country to Roman Catholicism. This was something the people would not tolerate and the so-called Glorious Revolution brought about James's downfall and replacement by the joint sovereigns, William III and Mary II. Mary, as James's daughter, was able to command the loyalty which her family had so long inspired, while her husband and cousin William (a Stuart on his mother's side) remained an uninspiring figure accepted as the champion of Protestantism and, after Mary's early death, was endured without enthusiasm until his own death brought Mary's sister Anne to the throne.

Anne's popularity mirrored that of Elizabeth I. She possessed the Stuart charisma in abundance and her tragic failure to rear any of her numerous children only served to endear her even more to her subjects. She would have liked the succession to revert to her Stuart half-brother, but the Act of Settlement had ensured the Protestant succession and Anne's death in 1714 brought the first Hanoverian monarch from Germany to claim the throne.

George I and George II were tolerated rather than loved and neither could be described as a popular monarch. George I's command of English was almost non-existent, while George II's, although fluent, was so heavily accented as to be well-nigh unintelligible. The reigns of both were further marred by the unedifying quarrels which both pursued with his heir apparent.

With the accession of George III in 1760, a new phase in the history of the royal family began. The young King, as he himself said in his first speech to parliament, 'gloried in the name of Briton', having been born and bred in England with English as his first language. The young German princess whom he married in the year after his succession soon adapted herself to her new country and the simple, uncomplicated tastes of the King and Queen and their fast growing young family endeared them to the British public in a way which none of their predecessors had achieved. The royal family adopted a lifestyle more in keeping with that of the emerging middle class rather than that of the old aristocracy, with whom they had little in common. Plain fare was served at the royal table and a plain style of dress was affected by the sovereigns, although they could rise to the occasion for court functions and great state ceremonies, which were not to their natural inclination. It was probably because of their austere upbringing that George III's sons did their best to reverse the situation by their louche and often flamboyant behaviour.

George IV, as Regent and King, brought about a brief return of royal magnificence and grandeur with his self-importance and great sense of showmanship. It is only today that we have come to realise how much we owe to his exquisite taste and connoisseurship in the arts. In his day, he was one of our most unpopular sovereigns, reviled for the scandals in his private life as much as for his extravagance. The brief reign of his brother and successor, William IV, a bluff and hearty sailor whose wilder eccentricities were tempered by the gentle influence of Queen Adelaide, paved the way for the accession of Queen Victoria, in whose reign royal popularity was to reach its zenith.

Although Victoria had to weather some anti-monarchical demonstrations during the early years of her reign, she won through with Albert's guidance and despite her later years of seclusion as 'the widow of Windsor' was to end it as the most loved monarch this country has known. 'Well done, old girl,' the spontaneous exclamation of a bystander at her Diamond Jubilee procession, was music to her ears and greatly appreciated by her.

The short reign of Edward VII which followed that of Victoria again brought Britain a sovereign whose lifestyle and love of splendour emulated that of George IV to some extent, yet 'King Teddy' enjoyed a personal popularity second to none and his subjects were willing to turn a blind eye to his extramarital peccadilloes as was his wife, the beautiful Queen Alexandra.

Under King George V and Queen Mary, the royal family returned to the humdrum, though much admired, domesticity effected by George III and Victoria. At his

The monarchy will survive because history has shown it to be the most stable form of government where the head of state is above politics and provides continuity whatever governments may come and go

Silver Jubilee in 1935 King George felt able to record in his diary after the overwhelming demonstration of popular affection he had received, 'I'd no idea they felt like that about me. I am beginning to think they must really like me for myself.'

The Abdication Crisis of 1936, far from weakening the monarchy as many predicted, only served to give it a new boost of popularity as King George VI and Queen Elizabeth continued the pattern set by King George V and Queen Mary, and the accession of a young and attractive Queen in 1952 was the occasion of further popular acclaim. Throughout her long reign, Queen Elizabeth II has maintained her personal popularity and on the occasion of her Silver Jubilee in 1977 the atmosphere which could be felt by anyone who mingled with the crowds testified to this a thousandfold. It is unfortunate that the matrimonial troubles experienced by the Queen's three married children have brought about a certain disillusionment in them and consequent loss of popularity, although Princess Anne appears to have suffered the least from this and a recent survey named her as the first choice for president should this country become a republic.

The monarchy will survive because history has shown it to be the most stable form of government where the head of state is above politics and provides continuity whatever governments may come and go, thus remaining the true representative of all the people. I am confident that when Queen Elizabeth II celebrates her Golden Jubilee in 2002 she will experience a demonstration of her people's love and affection exceeding that of 1977. Over the past 500 years, as I have tried to demonstrate, the popularity of our sovereigns and royal family has waxed and waned and it will continue to do so. If the Queen matches her mother's longevity the next reign may be comparatively short, but I venture to predict that the monarchy will enjoy a new golden age under the future King William V.

© *Manorial Society of Great Britain January, 1998*

Public swings in favour of the Prince

Charles's popularity rivals Blair's. By Peter Riddell

The Prince of Wales has become as popular as Tony Blair after a big swing of public opinion in his favour since the death of Diana, Princess of Wales, according to a MORI poll for *The Times*.

The poll, undertaken earlier this month, shows that more than three-fifths of the public are satisfied with the way Prince Charles is doing his job with fewer than three in ten dissatisfied. This is the same balance as for Mr Blair. Despite a drop in the Prime Minister's ratings over the past month, these figures are higher than those achieved by Margaret Thatcher at any time in her premiership.

These findings suggest that the public generally approves of the changed way that the Prince has handled his public appearances and his relations with his sons, Princes William and Harry, since their mother's death on August 31.

The precise figures are 61 per cent satisfied with the Prince and 29 dissatisfied, compared with 61 to 27 per cent for Mr Blair. But as recently as August, just before the death of the Princess, more people (46 per cent) were dissatisfied than satisfied (42 per cent) with the Prince.

The Prince of Wales has improved his ratings most among those aged over 55, with the middle classes and with Labour voters. His appeal seems to be strongest among the same non-Tory middle classes that have swung behind Mr Blair in the past couple of years. Mr Blair has higher approval ratings among men, the working class and 18 to 54-year-olds than the Prince.

The Queen enjoys the highest approval ratings. Nearly three-quarters, 72 per cent, say they are satisfied with the way she is doing her job with a fifth, 21 per cent, dissatisfied. Approval of the Queen rises with age, from 58 per cent among 18 to 24-year-olds to 83 per cent among pensioners, and is higher among middle than working classes, and among Tory than Labour supporters.

> **More than three-fifths of the public are satisfied with the way Prince Charles is doing his job with fewer than three in ten dissatisfied. This is the same balance as for Mr Blair**

The monarchy retains strong public approval, with only a small minority of republicans. Just 15 per cent think Britain would be better off if the monarchy were abolished, while 55 per cent say it would be worse off, and 27 per cent think it would make no difference. This represents a small swing in favour of the monarchy since September.

The new balance believing that Britain would be worse off if the monarchy were abolished is now higher than over the past four years, though it is lower than during the late 1980s before all the controversy started over the break-up of the marriages of Prince Charles and Prince Andrew.

There are sharp contrasts in attitudes to the monarchy among various social groups. The largest number believing that Britain would be better off if the monarchy were abolished are in Wales (27 per cent), among the unemployed (25 per cent) and readers of *The Guardian* (32 per cent) and *The Independent* (26 per cent). Readers of tabloid papers are, in general, more supportive of the monarchy than the average.

Satisfaction with the way Prince Charles is doing his job as Prince of Wales is highest among readers of *The Daily Telegraph* (72 per cent), *The Times* and *Daily Mail* (69 per cent), *Daily Express* (68 per cent) and *The Sun* (64).

- MORI interviewed 2,122 adults on December 12 to 15 at 169 sampling points across Britain.

ADDITIONAL RESOURCES

You might like to contact the following organisations for further information. Due to the increasing cost of postage, many organisations cannot respond to enquiries unless they receive a stamped, addressed envelope.

A Regal Reader
10 Ongar Road
London, SW6 1RJ
Tel: 0171 385 3551
A bookseller of second-hand and antiquarian books on the subject of the monarchy, worldwide. Deals with mail-order and catalogue orders. Has selections of its book list at The London Antiquarian Book Arcade, 37 Great Russell Street, London, WC1B 3PP.

Australian Republican Movement (ARM)
PO Box 16274
London, W2 1ZP
Tel: 0171 886 1667
The central aim of the Australian Republican Movement, which was launched in July 1991, is that Australia's Head of State becomes an Australian citizen chosen by Australians by the end of this century.

Australians for Constitutional Monarchy (ACM)
PO Box R903
Royal Exchange
N.S.W. 2000.
Australia
Tel: 00 02 241 2816
Fax: 00 02 247 5579
To answer the formation of the Australian Republican Movement and the unanimous resolution of the Australian Labor Party both pressing for a republic in Australia by the end of the century, a group of Australians came together to defend their constitution and preserve the Australian Crown from such attacks.

Buckingham Palace Press Office
London
Tel: 0171 930 4832
See their web site (details on page 43).

Foreign & Commonwealth Office
King Charles' Street
London, SW1A 2AH
Tel: 0171 270 1500
Fax: 0171 839 2417
The mission of the Foreign & Commonwealth Office is to promote the national interest of the UK and to contribute to a strong world community.

Majesty Magazine
26-28 Hallam Street
London, W1N 2NP
Tel: 0171 436 4006
Majesty Magazine is a full-colour A4 monthly publication produced by Rex Publications costing £2.50 per copy. The content includes the royal engagements from Buckingham Palace and European news. It also sells books and memorabilia. The number to call to subscribe is 01858 468888.

Republic
PO Box 2968
London, W14 9ZT
Tel: 0181 947 7427
Republic is an independent pressure group – not connected to any political party – which campaigns to end to all forms of hereditary office. Republicans believe that the monarchy is out-dated and undemocratic and should be replaced by an elected Head of State. Republic has a growing membership and according to the latest polls the support of 33% of Britons.

Republican Democratic Group
PO Box 1161
London
Anti-monarchy organisation.
Faction of Socialist Workers Group

Royalty Digest: A Journal of Record
Church Street
Ticehurst
East Sussex, TN5 7AA
Tel: 01580 201 221
Fax: 01580 200 957
Pro-Monarchist publication.

Socialist Equality Party
PO Box 1306
Sheffield, S9 3UW
Tel: 0114 244 3545
Fax: 0114 244 0224
The Socialist Equality Party is the British section of the Fourth International – the world party of socialist revolution founded by Leon Trotsky in 1938. The SEP stands for the abolition of the profit system ad the rational utilisation of the world resources in the interests of ordinary people.

The Constitutional Monarchy Association
PO Box 430
Chingford, E4 9SQ
Tel: 0181 531 4616
A pro-monarchy organisation.

The Manorial Society of Great Britain
104 Kennington Road
London, SE11 6RE
Tel: 0171 735 6633
Fax: 0171 582 7022
Founded in 1906 The Manorial Society of Great Britain promotes the study of English History and traditions, especially the Monarchy and British Parliamentary institutions. Founded in 1906

The Monarchist League
BM "Monarchist"
London
WC1N 3XX
Tel: 01892 835899
Pro-Monarchy organisation founded in 1943 to 'celebrate, preserve and promote the monarchical form of government'.

INDEX

The Internet has been likened to shopping in a supermarket without aisles. The press of a button on a Web browser can bring up thousands of sites but working your way through them to find what you want can involve long and frustrating on-line searches. And unfortunately many sites contain inaccurate, misleading or heavily biased information. Our researchers have therefore undertaken an extensive analysis to bring you a selection of quality Web site addresses. If our readers feel that this new innovation in the series is useful, we plan to provide a more extensive Web site section in each new book in the *Issues* series.

* * * * *

Australian Republic Unplugged
www.statusquo.org
The Australian Republic Unplugged web site provides an in-depth look at the republic debate in Australia.

Australian Republican Movement (ARM)
www.republic.org.au
The central aim of the Australian Republican Movement is that Australia's Head of State becomes an Australian citizen chosen by Australians by the end of this century.

Buckingham Palace Press Office
The Royal Web site can be found at www.royal.gov.uk The 150-page Royal Web site is illustrated throughout. The Royal Web site also includes a section dealing with the most frequently asked questions put to Buckingham Palace by members of the public in this country and overseas and a feedback form on the Web site, designed as a 'visitors' book', which will provide the necessary feedback to ensure that the site is meeting the information requirements of Internet users.

Charter 88
http://www.charter88.org.uk
This site contains information on matters relating to political reform in the UK.

Monarchy web sites of general interest
Web sites which may be of interest to monarchist cyber surfers are listed below:
Danish Royal Court: www.kongehuset.dk
Swedish Royal Court: www.royalcourt.se
K Z-M (Polish monarchists): www.man.poznan.pl~bielecki/kzmen.htm
FERT (Italian monarchists): www.vol.it/fede_monarc/
Constitutional Movement of Iran: www.irancmi.org
Brazilian Monarchist Movement: www.arsa.com/monarquia
Swazi Royal Court: www.pitt.edu:80/~tgsst10/swaziland.E.html

Republic
www.mrm.co.uk
Republic is an independent pressure group – not connected to any political party – which campaigns to end to all forms of hereditary office.

The Canadian Government
www.canada.gc.ca/royalvisit.
A bilingual (English/French) web site devoted to the role the Queen discharges as Sovereign of Canada.

* * * * * *

ACKNOWLEDGEMENTS

The publisher is grateful for permission to reproduce the following material.

While every care has been taken to trace and acknowledge copyright, the publisher tenders its apology for any accidental infringement or where copyright has proved untraceable. The publisher would be pleased to come to a suitable arrangement in any such case with the rightful owner.

Chapter One: The Role of the Monarchy

The monarchy, © Charter 88, July 1998, *The Queen's role in the modern state*, © Buckingham Palace Press Office, *Royal finances*, © Buckingham Palace Press Office, *The Commonwealth*, © Buckingham Palace Press Office, *The Queen's role in the Commonwealth*, © Buckingham Palace Press Office.

Chapter Two: The Monarchy Debate

The case for the monarchy, © The Monarchist League, *Some say the monarchy should change in light of Diana's death*, © The Sunday Times/NOP poll, *The press and the Monarchy*, © Roy Greenslade / Republic, 1996, *Do you think the monarchy will exist in its present form in 30 years' time?*, © The Sunday Times/NOP poll, *Watchdogs to scrutinise royal finances*, © The Independent, December 1997, *Don't ask the Queen to change*, © The Daily Mail, September 1997, *The British Royal Family*, © MORI, January 1997, *Off with their heads*, © The Socialist Review, *Should Royals bow to reform?*, © Times Newspapers Limited, March 1998, *Towards a British Republic*, © Republic, *Actually, the people these few weeks have been bad for are the republicans*, © The Spectator, September 1997, *Who would you like to see succeed the Queen?*, © The Sunday Times/NOP poll, *House of Windsor split over new look*, © The Independent, March 1998, *The Queen torn over reforms*, © The Mail on Sunday, March 1998, *Soames hails Royal Family's staying power*, © Telegraph Group Limited, London 1998, *Half favour William as next King*, © Telegraph Group Limited, London 1997, *Remote and stuffy royals must change*, © The Observer, September 1997, *Verdict on the monarchy*, © Observer/ICM, *Queen to move out of Palace*, © The Independent on Sunday, November 1997, *Embattled Royal Family may reduce its ranks*, © Telegraph Group Limited, London 1997, *The saving of the monarchy*, © The Guardian, September 1997, *Some say the Queen is in touch with the feelings of the British people, others say she is remote and out of touch . . .*, © The Sunday Times/NOP poll, *Royal Family is regaining public esteem*, © Telegraph Group Limited London, 1997, *% saying opinion of Royal Family has 'gone up'*, © The Sunday Times/NOP poll, *A word from two groups*, © Australians for Constitutional Monarchy and The Australian Republic Movement, *Mounted opposition*, © Republic, *You must earn your keep, Royals told*, © The Mail on Sunday, March, 1998, *The Civil List*, © The Mail on Sunday, March, 1998, *If I were the Why the Queen should abdicate . . .*, © The Independent on Sunday, March 1998, *Should the Queen continue on the throne until the end of her life, step down at 75 or step down now?*, © The Sunday Times/NOP poll, *Why the monarchy will survive*, © Manorial Society of Great Britain, January 1998, *Has Diana's death strengthened or weakened your support for the monarchy?*, © The Sunday Times/NOP poll, *Public swings in favour of the Prince*, © Times Newspapers Limited, December 1997.

Photographs and illustrations:

Pages 1, 5, 7, 8, 13, 16: The Attic Publishing Co., pages 10, 14, 22, 27, 32, 40: Ken Pyne.

Thank you

Darin Jewell for assisting in the editorial research for this publication.

Craig Donnellan
Cambridge
September, 1998